THE
INTERIOR
DESIGN
DIRECTORY

A SOURCEBOOK OF MODERN MATERIALS

ELIZABETH WILHIDE

QUADRILLE

contents

introduction

Opposite: Many materials, both natural and synthetic, have an inherent affinity with one another, which makes it easy to create a decorative scheme.

Until fairly recently, the choices people made when it came to decorating their homes were largely articulated in terms of things – furniture, lamps, curtains, rugs, pictures and objects – as well as domestic kit and equipment, such as pots and pans, plates and glasses, which accompany everyday life. Increasingly, however, the focus has shifted onto the material quality of interior spaces – what's on the walls, what the floor is made of, along with details such as fitted counters and worktops, cladding, doors and windows. Backgrounds are no longer boring blank planes to be painted or papered over: they have become the means by which the particular character of an interior can be expressed.

This approach is invariably less superficial than more transient forms of decoration that can be changed as fashion or taste dictates. It requires a certain degree of investment; it brings various practical issues into play; it takes the long view. But the commitment is well worth while. Evocative combinations of materials – glass and metal, concrete and wood – have an inherent vitality that directs attention to basic elements of design, such as the way light falls across a floor or the interplay of architectural forms. It is not a question of backgrounds screaming for attention, rather that in speaking for themselves, materials used as surfaces and finishes create a rooted sense of physicality that grounds our perception of space.

Opposite: New materials are emerging all the time. This vivid plastic sheeting was produced from recycled plastic bottles.

Materials have always played a role in the decoration of homes, but what has changed has been both the way in which they are used and the breadth of choice now open to us. In the past, the repertoire of surfaces and finishes was relatively narrow and predictable, and variety was delivered more superficially through pattern and applied finish or decoration. Today, when we think about selecting flooring, for example, we can draw on a whole range of materials – from glass to metal to concrete – that have practically no history of domestic use at all. Equally important, when we choose a particular surface, is that we expect by and large to reveal it: if we choose a wooden countertop, we want to see the warm, rich grain; if we opt for concrete, it is the raw brute material that defines the aesthetic, not its potential to be covered up. In the same way, traditional applications have also been challenged. Stone is not merely found underfoot, but cladding baths. Hardwood veneer is not restricted to cabinetry, but lines whole walls. Plastics are not confined to the cheap, disposable or utilitarian applications, but find new and expressive uses as glowing backlit screens and panels.

A growing interest in material quality has gone hand in hand with contemporary design. In one way, this is perfectly understandable. We surround ourselves with fewer worldly goods and furnish our homes more minimally than previous generations, which naturally means that the basic elements of floors, walls, windows and so on become

This page: The urban loft, with its vast expanses of space and industrial aesthetic, has had a profound influence on our use of materials in the home.

much more important thanks to their sheer visibility. At the same time, ever since the first loft was colonized in the 1970s, more and more homes have been fashioned from redundant buildings that once served very different purposes. Focusing on material quality is an obvious way of meeting the challenge of designing and decorating a space that was formerly a warehouse, a factory, a church or a school.

Materials bring with them a whole raft of associations, not only because of their innate characteristics but also their history of use. One obvious distinction that has long been made is between materials that are costly and rare and those that are common and cheap, with the former spelling out power and status. In the past, people worked by and large with what was to hand – local timber, and stone, brick and tile where there were deposits of clay – while the materials in short supply, or those that had to be imported, were solely the preserve of the rich. Yet long before plastics appeared on the scene, simulation of expensive surfaces and finishes – in paint, for example – was

Opposite: Tiles have always been a
practical choice for bathroom flooring.
This ceramic tiling with its striated
pattern has great depth of character.

beginning to erode this seemingly hard-and-fast distinction. You can see the same process at work today. With increasingly sophisticated simulations of wood, stone, tile and other 'natural' materials on the market, the exclusivity of a 'luxury' finish such as marble has suffered somewhat by comparison. Or, to give another example, strong colour, formerly the product of expensive pigments and dyes, was once only for the wealthy and was a true signifier of status. In the post-war period, developments in plastics technology meant that bright colours were suddenly everywhere – on walls, printed fabric, and cheap, disposable plastic goods of all kinds. What had been a hallmark of luxury was now 'cheap and cheerful'.

Another opposition has been between 'natural' and 'artificial' or 'synthetic'. Ever since the Arts and Crafts movement placed the honest expression of materials at the forefront of the design agenda, materials that are derived from organic or earthen sources have been valued above those that are the products of manufacture, a preference that has acquired a moral imperative recently because of increased ecological concerns. Yet, again, the picture is by no means clear cut. In the right context, for example, a material such as steel, which is highly processed and has high embodied energy, can be a better and more sustainable choice than one that is, to all intents and purposes, wholly natural.

Today we are entering a whole new phase, as technology advances in leaps and bounds and, in the process, redefines what a 'material' actually is. Stone, cloth, bricks, wood, steel – these are what most people understand as materials. They have a host of measurable physical characteristics that shape how they are worked, how they perform, and what they look and feel like. But what about composites engineered out of many different materials, some of which may be natural and some of which may not? Or concrete you can see through? Or glass that cleans itself? Or wall tiles embedded with LEDs? Or fabric that grows a pattern in response to light levels? Are they materials, or products or applications of technology – or all three?

In some cases, these examples from the new generation of materials have been developed to solve a particular problem. For example, the expanses of glazing that are a feature of much modern design can cause excessive heat loss or gain. The solution – insulating glass coated with a thin layer of metal oxide – represents a direct attempt to address a shortfall in basic practicality. In other cases, a material/product/technical application has come about simply because a designer or artist has put two seemingly unrelated things together for the fun of it – fabric and photochromic inks, for example, or digital printing and ceramic tile. Just as Formica was originally developed for electrical insulation but found a home on kitchen counters and tabletops across the

world, many material innovations that started out as specialist solutions in nondomestic contexts have found more expressive applications because someone has thought creatively about their design potential. As old-style materials, which are worked mechanically, give way to electronic ones that have the potential to respond to their environment, the boundaries are likely to become more and more blurred.

The Interior Design Directory is a compendium of materials for home design – from the familiar to the cutting edge. What it is, where to get it, what to do with it – each material has its own comprehensive, accessible entry. While for ease of reference the book is divided into four main sections – Classic, Contemporary, Smart and Sustainable – what is clear is that materials will always resist simple categorization, no matter how much we try to pigeonhole them. In the end, what really matters is how they are used and what value – both aesthetic and practical – they bring to our lives.

classic

classic
introduction

What makes a material a classic? For one thing, time: many of the surfaces and finishes that fall into this category have been part of the domestic fabric of our homes for centuries. Wood, stone, tiles, carpets and rugs are as familiar to us as the concept of home itself.

What many classic materials provide is depth of character, a whole package of sensory experiences bound up in a single surface or finish – the smooth, dense chill of stone; the resilience of wood with its irregular pattern of grain; the softness and tactility of woven textiles. This richness of experience sets up associations that are often linked to a particular application – wooden or stone flooring, for example, or draped fabric hanging at the window. We seek out these materials time and again, not simply because we know they will deliver, but also because we value the continuity they offer. Since many of these materials are wholly natural, they age gracefully, improving with use and wear.

A classic material used in a standard application exudes quiet confidence. It does not call attention to itself but promotes a sense of wellbeing that is reassuring and hospitable. And most, if not all, classic materials work well in different surroundings – from period homes to modern apartments; their very familiarity makes them supremely adaptable.

On the practical side, because these materials have such a long history of use, there is a wealth of information available: how a material behaves under various conditions, the right means of fixing it and the best way to look after it will have been established over years of application. By and large, it won't be difficult to source the material or to find the right expertise to install it. Safe in the knowledge that you aren't venturing into the unknown, you can focus on its aesthetic properties – its colour, patterning or textural qualities – and make your selection according to the effect you want to create.

What, then, are the downsides? Some might say this family of materials can be a little too safe and self-effacing, perhaps even a bit boring. And because there are so many synthetic versions of these materials on the market, the integrity of the real thing can become a little eroded. Yet often all that is required to give a classic material a new lease of life is to use it in a less expected way. A bath clad in stone tiles, for example, or a wall lined in a beautiful hardwood veneer, are the type of applications that lift a classic material out of the ordinary and restore its inherent vitality.

Above: A mosaic-tiled bathroom with a glass shower screen.

This page: Classic hardwood flooring in light-toned ash.

wood

Wood is one of the most versatile of all natural materials and has been employed in the construction, decoration and furnishing of our houses since time immemorial. From beams, rafters and studwork partitions to panelling, flooring, mouldings, frames and furniture, wood serves many functions, both seen and unseen.

Of the 40,000 or so known species of tree, only around 30 are in common use for wood, and these display a remarkable variety, not merely in terms of appearance, but also in basic properties and characteristics. The two main types are softwoods and hardwoods, though these categories are far from precise. Manufactured woods, also included in this section, contain different amounts of timber or timber waste formed into solid boards using heat, pressure, glues and other additives.

Although wood derives from a living renewable resource, its use is associated with certain environmental problems. While in theory it ought to be possible to plant a tree for every tree that is logged, demand still outstrips supply. Deforestation – to clear land for agriculture as well as to satisfy the requirements of the timber industry – has decimated many ancient forests worldwide. These are not renewable, nor are the unique habitats they provide for endangered species. Wood is also commonly transported great distances, which adds to its environmental impact.

It is essential to acquire timber only from accredited sustainable sources, the more local the better. The Forestry Stewardship Council (FSC) monitors forestry projects around the world to protect endangered species and to safeguard the livelihoods and traditions of local communities. While certain species of tree are under threat in some areas, boycotting is not usually the answer as it may encourage deforestation by devaluing the timber, while precluding the acquisition of the same timber from a properly managed forest.

Sourcing wood responsibly
• Buy wood from sustainable managed plantations. Look for certification from the FSC, the PEFC (Programme for the Endorsement of Forest Certification) or similar bodies.
• Buy locally if possible. Local timber has less far to travel, reducing its environmental impact. Otherwise, look at the supplier's environmental performance.
• A small number of timber species are banned. These are listed by the Convention on International Trade in Endangered Species of Wildlife and Flora (CITES).
• Threatened tropical hardwoods include mahogany, teak, sapele, merbau, ebony, iroko, keruing and wenge.
• Don't insist on the highest grade of timber (which is only found in the heartwood). This reduces waste.
• Use salvaged or reclaimed wood whenever possible.

Timber terms
Wood is worked in a variety of ways, which affects its appearance and sometimes its durability.

Plain sawn Timber cut parallel along the length of the trunk. Boards display the greatest variety of graining patterns and colour, and the highest number of knots.

Quarter-sawn Timber that is cut radially. Boards are more uniform in colour and texture.

End grain Timber cut against the grain. Boards are dense and durable. End-grain wood can be jointed or glued together to make larger surfaces or used for parquet.

Sapwood New wood containing living cells. Light, porous and prone to rotting.

Heartwood The most select grade cut from the central portion. Boards are largely free of defects and marking.

Veneer Extremely thin sheets of timber cut to reveal graining and colour. Veneers from beautiful hardwoods are commonly applied to softwood carcases, panels or bases for decoration, or to suggest a more expensive product.

Green wood Unseasoned timber, or timber that has not been dried, either naturally or artificially. Green oak can be used to create timber-framed structures.

Seasoned wood Wood is dried to a moisture content of 10 per cent, as recommended for indoor use. During seasoning, wood contracts principally across its width, but also along its length. Artificial seasoning in a kiln dries wood at an even rate, preventing warping and splitting.

1

2

hardwood

While the distinction between hardwood and softwood is less clear cut than might be commonly supposed, hardwoods as a group tend to be much more varied in appearance, with many displaying highly attractive colours, grain and patterning. They come from both temperate and tropical areas, and from both deciduous and evergreen broad-leaved trees. They are also comparatively expensive. Some types are rare, and trading is prohibited in the case of a small number of tropical timbers that are in serious decline. The most durable hardwoods come from tropical areas.

Hardwood flooring is available in the form of solid boards or planks of varying widths, as well as in shorter strips or blocks that can be pieced together in different patterns to create a parquet floor. Another common use of hardwoods is as veneers covering softwood panels, bases or carcases.

Afrormosia
Appearance: Dark-toned, becoming darker on exposure; fine texture; straight grain.
Characteristics: Very durable; restricted availability.
Applications: Exterior and interior carpentry, furniture, flooring.

Afzelia
Appearance: Mid-toned; coarse texture.
Characteristics: Very durable; readily polished.
Applications: Exterior and interior carpentry, flooring.

Ash (varieties: American Ash, European Ash)
Appearance: Typically pale; coarse texture; straight grain.
Characteristics: Medium hard; tough; extremely flexible.
Applications: Veneers for cabinetry or cladding, flooring, furniture.

Beech
Appearance: Light colour; uniform straight grain.
Characteristics: Medium hard; strong; easy to work and bend.
Applications: Flooring, cabinetry, cladding, bentwood furniture.

Birch (varieties: American Birch, European Birch)
Appearance: Pale colour with straight grain (European); pale with whorled figuring (American).
Characteristics: Medium hard; not particularly strong.
Applications: Plywood, veneers, furniture, finish carpentry.

Cherry (varieties: American Cherry, European Cherry)
Appearance: Darkens on exposure (American); fine, even, straight grain.
Characteristics: Easy to work and bend.
Applications: Furniture, flooring (American), contrasting borders, veneers.

3

4

5

Chestnut

Appearance: Lightish colour; slightly wavy grain.

Characteristics: Soft; naturally resistant to pests and fungus.

Applications: Flooring, cabinetry, finish carpentry.

1. Hardwood cladding on mezzanine.
2. Ash.
3. Birch.
4. 'Rust'-toned beech.
5. Beech.
6. Cherry.

6

1

2

3

Elm (American)
Appearance: Mid-toned; medium grain.
Characteristics: Not durable; only available in small sections.
Applications: Interior carpentry, furniture.

Eucalyptus (also known as jarrah)
Appearance: Mid- to light-toned; wavy grain.

Characteristics: Resinous; medium hard; durability dependent on variety.
Applications: Flooring, interior carpentry.

Iroko
Appearance: Similar to teak; straight grain.
Characteristics: Medium hard; extremely durable.
Applications: Exterior and interior carpentry, worktops, flooring, veneers, cabinetry, teak substitute.

Ironwood
Appearance: Warm colour; fine twisted grain.
Characteristics: Very hard and durable.
Applications: Stairs, veneers, floors, furniture, cabinetry.

Jatoba (Brazilian cherry)
Appearance: Warm-toned; fine grain.
Characteristics: Exceptionally hard, almost twice as hard as white oak.
Applications: Furniture, flooring, decorative veneers.

Keruing
Appearance: Dark-toned; coarse texture.

4

5

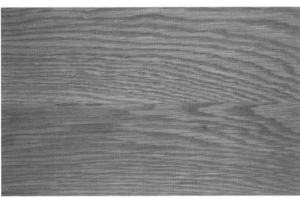

6

squash courts, bowling
alleys), furniture.

Merbau

Appearance: Similar to
mahogany; straight or
twisted grain.
Characteristics: Oily surface;
very hard and durable.
Applications: Exterior and
interior carpentry, flooring,
veneers, furniture, cabinetry.

Oak (many varieties)

Appearance: Pale or mid-
brown, darkening to velvety
grey with weathering; coarse,
open grain.
Characteristics: Very hard and
durable; difficult to carve and
work; easily split or cleft.
Applications: Structural
elements, flooring, interior
and exterior carpentry,
cabinetry, furniture.

1. Wide planking in jarrah.
2. Iroko.
3. Maple.
4. Jatoba
5. Wide oak boarding laid
as ship's decking.
6. Oak.

Characteristics: Durable;
available in long boards.
Applications: Construction,
exterior carpentry.

Mahogany (varieties: African
Mahogany, American Mahogany)

Appearance: Dark and richly
coloured, fine grain.
Characteristics: Strong;
naturally resistant to pests and
woodworm; easy to carve.

Applications: Flooring, furniture,
interior carpentry, veneers.

Maple

Appearance: Near-white; fine
even texture; straight grain.
Characteristics: Medium hard;
very durable and wear-resistant;
good for steam-bending.
Applications: Flooring in
areas where there is heavy
traffic (dance halls, gymnasia,

1

2

3

Padauk
Appearance: Dark red colour; straight grain.
Characteristics: Easy to work and carve; very durable.
Applications: Exterior and interior carpentry, furniture.

Sapele
Appearance: Mid-toned; fine grain; similar to mahogany.
Characteristics: Medium hard; fairly durable.
Applications: Exterior and interior carpentry, veneers, furniture, cabinetry.

Sycamore
Appearance: Creamy white; straight grain.
Characteristics: Medium hard; easy to work and steam-bend.
Applications: Furniture, flooring, veneers, cabinetry.

Teak
Appearance: Mid- to dark-toned; coarse texture; straight grain.
Characteristics: Very durable; highly weather-resistant thanks to oiliness.
Applications: Decking, outdoor and indoor furniture, external carpentry.

Tulipwood
Appearance: Very pale; straight grain.
Characteristics: Very soft; not durable.
Applications: Plywood, veneers, furniture, cabinetry.

Walnut
Appearance: Beautifully figured and dark-toned; coarse texture; straight or wavy grain; may

4

5

6

7

have cracks or knots.
Characteristics: Prone to
woodworm; easy to work.
Applications: Flooring, veneers,
furniture, joinery.

Wenge

Appearance: Very dark;
straight grain.
Characteristics: Very hard;
durable.
Applications: Exterior and

interior carpentry, floors,
veneers, cabinetry.

1. Wenge breakfast bar.
2. Wenge has a very
straight grain.
3. Wenge kitchen counter.
4. Walnut kitchen counter.
5. Detail of walnut finish.
6. Teak.
7. Walnut is noted for the
beauty of its figuring.

2

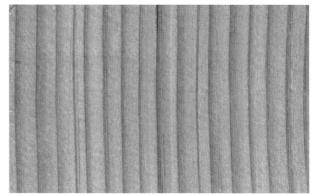

1

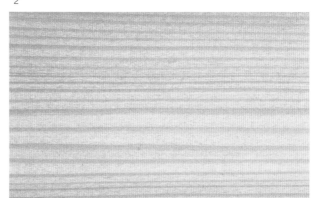

3

softwood

Softwoods, which derive from coniferous or needle-leaved trees, are far less varied as a group than hardwoods and are typically pale, close-grained and knotty. Most softwood species are native to temperate regions, such as the northern United States, Canada, Scandinavia, Britain, Russia and other parts of the former Soviet Union, with the cooler and more northerly areas producing trees of higher quality. Most softwoods are less dense than hardwoods, though Douglas fir is just as hard as African mahogany.

Timber from softwoods tends to be used for utilitarian purposes – in construction, joinery and carpentry and other behind-the-scenes applications.

As a basic material in high demand, it is widely available pre-cut to various standard sizes and formats, including structural timbers, boards or planks, and profile boards (tongue-and-groove matched boards). While certain hardwoods are naturally resistant to rot and pests, all softwood must be treated before use.

Unlike hardwoods, whose sourcing continues to be controversial and problematic, most softwoods today come from managed plantations, with certain large retailers – IKEA among them – guaranteeing to obtain wood only from certified suppliers. Compared with hardwoods, softwood species are relatively fast-growing, with

trees reaching sufficient size for logging after 60 years or so.

'Pine' is often used as a generic term for softwood timber. In fact, there are a number of different varieties of pine, as well as other coniferous species that produce softwood timber.

Cedar of Lebanon
Appearance: Pale tone; knotty.
Characteristics: Strong aromatic smell; durable.
Application: Interior carpentry.

Douglas fir
Appearance: Attractive grain.
Characteristics: Resinous; fairly durable; long boards available.
Application: Exterior and interior carpentry, furniture.

European silver fir
Appearance: Numerous small knots.
Characteristics: Not durable; easy to work.
Application: All-purpose construction timber, furniture, glulam beams.

Larch
Appearance: Knotty; wavy grain.
Characteristics: Resinous; medium hard; not durable.
Application: Flooring, plywood, veneers.

Norway spruce
Appearance: Pale; straight grain.
Characteristics: Medium hard; not durable.
Application: Interior carpentry, glulam beams.

4

Scots pine (redwood)
Appearance: Pale to reddish; knotty.
Characteristics: Not durable; available in long boards; abundant; easy to work.
Application: General construction and joinery.

Western hemlock
Appearance: Light in tone; straight grain.

Characteristics: Soft; wear-resistant.
Applications: Exterior and interior carpentry, cladding, saunas, veneers.

Western red cedar
Appearance: Warm tone, weathers to grey; wavy grain.
Characteristics: Very soft; highly moisture- and rot-resistant; aromatic.

Applications: Exterior carpentry and garden use; shingles; interior carpentry.

Yellow pine
Appearance: Very light; fine, even, straight grain.
Characteristics: Very soft; not durable; dimensionally stable; easy to work.
Applications: Interior carpentry, doors, joinery, furniture.

1. Rustic pine beams.
2. Douglas fir.
3. Spruce.
4. Exterior of a pine lodge in California.

1

salvaged & reclaimed wood

The ultimate eco-friendly option is to use reclaimed or salvaged wood. At its most basic level, this may simply entail repairing and refinishing whatever wooden surfaces and finishes already exist in your home. Many older properties have timber floors, with boards running sideways from wall to wall over timber joists. These can be exposed, repaired, sanded and sealed for considerably less than the cost of a new hardwood floor.

Other sources of reclaimed wood include salvage yards and junk shops for original doors, panelling, cabinetry and other wooden fixtures and fittings. Antique parquet can be even more expensive than new, particularly if it is French and of known provenance. Some outlets supply reclaimed floorboards that have been denailed and remachined to preserve the character of the original surface.

1. Eco hunting lodge in Tasmania.
2. Reclaimed timber door.

2

1

manufactured wood & wood products

Manufactured woods, containing varying degrees of the natural material, including timber waste (what is left over after usable boards, planks and solid timbers have been cut), come in a wide range of specifications. Many are available as sheets or panels of a greater size than can be cut from a tree, some as exceptionally strong structural beams, while others take the form of familiar laminate flooring or cladding systems available in the mass-market. Most of these materials are cheap.

Plywood

Having made its first commercial appearance in the nineteenth century, plywood only began to come into its own in the early modern period when it was valued for its cool, utilitarian aesthetic. The material is composed of odd-numbered thin sheets of wood (or 'plies') laid at right angles to each other and glued together. This process of lamination delivers stability and makes the sheets less likely to warp than a sheet of the same size made of solid timber. Different thicknesses of plies and facing veneers are available, giving different edge profiles. Marine ply, which has enhanced water-resistance, is recommended as a subfloor in areas such as bathrooms and kitchens where damp is likely.

A variety of different woods are used to make plywood. Among the most common is either birch-faced or all-birch. Other common veneer or facing woods include Douglas fir or, more expensively, hardwoods such as maple, oak and teak. Very classy plywoods are composed of oak or beech plies, which produce attractive edging and facing.
Applications: As a subfloor or final flooring, panelling, partitions, tabletops, bent furniture.

Glulam

Glulam ('glued laminated') timber and beams are extremely strong structural members formed by gluing sheets, boards or planks of softwood together under pressure, with the grain running parallel. The resulting product is very stable and strong and is available in extra-long lengths to span greater distances.
Applications: Timber-frame construction, floors, roofs, ceilings.

Blockboard

A cheap utility material, blockboard consists of a core of solid wood strips glued together and sandwiched by face veneers or plies. It comes in a range of thicknesses and qualities; cut edges, however, are gappy and need to be covered with a facing strip if they are to be displayed.
Applications: Shelving for light loads, stair construction, furniture manufacture.

2

Fibreboard

This is made of fibre particles (chiefly wood) subjected to intense heat and pressure and generally combined with glues. One of the most common is MDF (medium density fibreboard), the ubiquitous ingredient of television makeover programmes. MDF is uniform, dimensionally stable and strong, and can be worked very precisely for a crisp, clean-lined look. It is also easy to decorate. A new type is available that is through-coloured. Standard MDF contains plastic resin that has environmental implications, but it is possible to source MDF that is formaldehyde-free. In either case, it is recommended that you wear a mask and goggles when working with the material to avoid inhaling the fine dust. Applications: Interior panels, furniture, cladding, cabinetry, subfloors.

Oriented strand board (OSB)

Made of coarse softwood chips arranged crosswise in layers or plies and pressed under heat, OSB is much stronger than chipboard and similar manufactured woods. Its rough, rather brutal aesthetic stems from the fact that it is most often seen as temporary external boarding. Applications: Interior cladding or panelling, external boarding or temporary weatherproofing.

Wood laminate

Technically, all the artificial woods and wood products described in this section are laminates in that they are composed of layers (of wood fibres, veneers, chips or solid timber) bonded together using a combination of heat, pressure, glues and resins. What are chiefly understood as laminate, however, are those interior wood products and systems designed to be used as flooring, panelling and worktops, or in the construction of fitted kitchens, bathrooms and other storage.

Composition of wood laminates varies. Generally, however, there will be an outer facing veneer applied to a core made of a number of different layers designed to promote various qualities, such as resilience, water-resistance and so on. In some cases, the outer veneer will be substantial enough to sand should it become worn or scratched; in mass-market versions, the outer 'veneer' may simply be paper printed to simulate a wood finish and covered with vinyl.

1. Child's bunkbed made of plywood.
2. Plywood screen in a living room.

2

1. Painted plywood fitted storage.
2. Kitchen units made of parallam,
a type of glulam.

function & format

Wood has one of the most varied ranges of applications of any material. It is so ubiquitous, in fact, that the challenge can be to use it in such a way that its essential character is enhanced and it makes a positive contribution to the feeling or mood of a space, rather than simply fades into the background.

Flooring

Wooden floors score highly for resilience, relative comfort and basic practicality. Cost varies: at the top end of the market are solid hardwood floors; at the lower end of the price spectrum are laminate floors that may be wood in name only.

• Solid hardwood floors are available in different widths. Wider boards (110mm to 490mm) are elegant and classy. Some wider boards consist of narrow strips glued together. Parquet (solid or veneered) comes in a range of patterns including herringbone and basketweave.

• 'Engineered' wooden floors consist of 3mm hardwood veneer applied over a softwood or plywood base. These floors are very stable and won't warp if used over underfloor heating.

• Most wooden floors are supplied pre-finished, either with lacquer, UV oil or some other sealant or treatment.

• Fitting solid floors is a professional's job. Fitting is done by secret nailing or by slotting boards together and fixing around the perimeter, leaving a small expansion gap to accommodate any future movement. Wood block may be glued down. Other proprietary systems that snap together can be fitted by a competent amateur.

• All wooden floors should be laid over a dry, even subfloor, such as plywood or hardboard. Wooden floors can be laid over concrete if the subfloor is covered with a damp-proof membrane and resilient underlay. It is advisable to use sound-insulating underlays in upper rooms to reduce impact sound.

• Skirtings, stair treads and risers are also available to match floors.

• Sheets of plywood make an attractive and economical floor, but don't expect it to last much more than about 10 years or so.

• The most durable external decking is made out of hardwood, typically teak or other naturally weather-resistant species. Pressure-treated softwood will last for a decent length of time provided it is regularly cleaned and cleared of moss. Wood-composite decking, cheap and long-lasting, consists of wood fibre mixed with vinyl.

Panelling and cladding

Lining a room or a wall in wood generates a sense of enclosure and intimacy.

• Traditional panelling features rectangular panels framed by horizontal rails and vertical stiles and is generally made of softwood stained to look like hardwood; hardwood panelling can also be commissioned from specialist suppliers.

• For a more homely, rustic effect, use matchboarding or tongue-and-groove panelling.

• Knotty pine cladding made of redwood is the unpretentious wall covering found in many American homes in the family or recreation room.

• A veneered panel can be used to pick out a wall or portion of a wall – such as an overscaled bedhead.

Fixtures and fittings

Other ways of using wood as a feature include:

• **Cantilevered stairs or shelving** Using thick sections of wood, cantilevered from the wall on invisible fixings, makes a bold statement.

• **Worksurfaces** Generally made from the heartwood of hardwoods such as beech and oak, with individual staves jointed together to make the desired width. Thickness varies from 2.5cm to 5cm. Usually supplied pre-finished with lacquer or oil.

• **Basins and baths** The ideal wood for this use is aromatic and antibacterial cedarwood. Beech, teak, wenge and birch are also used. Wooden baths must be used regularly or the wood will dry out and split.

Opposite: Painted wood wall panelling and exposed beams.

finishes & maintenance

Wood can last a very long time if it is looked after properly. Some woods, however, are naturally more resistant to deterioration than others. The oiliness of teak, for example, is what gives it such a high degree of weather-resistance, whereas nearly all softwoods will rot on exposure to damp without treatment.

Decorative finishes

Not all woods are equally absorbent – some will take a stain more readily than others. It is a good idea to test a section of wood to judge the effect before you commit yourself to a specific type of finish. Some types of wood – teak and other oily resinous hardwoods, for instance – don't take finishes at all.

• **Paint** Provides a high degree of coverage and offers a wide range of colours. Prime clean wooden surfaces with wood primer and then paint with oil-based top coat (eggshell or gloss). Hardwearing yacht or flooring paint is also available for painting floorboards.

• **Wood stain** Available in woody colours as well as other shades, wood stain sinks into the grain rather than obscures it. Both water- and spirit-based stains are available.

• **Bleaching** Wood can be 'limed' or bleached using any one of a number of proprietary products, or by rubbing gesso or some other type of white pigment into the grain. Bleaching knocks back the rather strident orangey tones of pine.

• **Darkening** Smoked and flamed finishes produce a darkening effect that deepens and enriches the tones of the wood.

Protective finishes

The main enemy of wood is damp. Most untreated wooden surfaces that get thoroughly soaked, or which suffer superficial damage so that moisture can penetrate, will rot and decay. Many wooden floors and worksurfaces are supplied ready-finished.

• **Preventative treatments for timber used in construction (usually softwood)** These include fungicides, insecticides and chemicals to promote fire-retardance. Natural alternatives include borax.

• **Varnishes and wood seals** These are often polyurethane-based and tend to yellow with age and exposure. Apply solvent-based varnishes with care, wearing protective clothing and keeping rooms well ventilated. Several coats may be needed for optimum protection. Varnishes need to be stripped and renewed after three years.

• **Oils** The traditional finish for hardwoods. Suitable oils include tung oil and teak oil.

• **Waxes** It is advisable to seal the wood first before waxing, or the wax will sink into the grain too readily.

• **Eco-friendly alternatives** These are generally water-based and chemical-free. Not as hardwearing as other types of finish.

Maintenance

• Keep wooden floors swept and vacuumed so that dirt and grit does not work its way through protective finishes.

• Wash wooden floors with a mild soapy cleanser that does not require rinsing.

• Avoid wearing stiletto heels, which will pock a wooden surface.

• Repair scratches or other areas of mild damage by sanding and refinishing.

1. Exposed wood ceiling and timber panelling.
2. Painted pine matchboarding cladding a staircase.

1

This page: Natural stone flooring has a rugged quality that can be emphasized by laying in irregular slabs.

stone

A classic material if there ever was one, stone carries with it a weight of associations that derive from its rich and varied history of use. Depending on the type of stone and how it is worked and applied, it can be refined or rustic, traditional or cutting edge, luxurious or down to earth. Whatever the setting, however, it always suggests permanence and continuity: it is there for the duration.

Stone is a heavy, dense material. Its massiveness means that it is slow to gain heat and slow to lose it, which makes it an ideal material for homes designed around passive solar strategies. In southern parts of Europe, for example, thick masonry walls and stone floors absorb heat slowly during the warm months and radiate it back into the interior during the winter. In northern areas stone flooring works well with underfloor heating; otherwise, its chilliness may be less welcome.

Stone is also exceptionally hard and unyielding. Objects that are dropped onto a stone floor or counter are more likely to break than not. Stone can also amplify sound to a considerable degree. Some types of stone are prone to staining and are unsuitable for certain types of application as a result.

The heaviness of the material means that floors or extensive stone surfaces, such as worksurfaces, may need additional support. A preliminary survey or expert guidance may need to be obtained to establish whether frameworks or subfloors can bear the additional weight. Stone almost always requires expert installation, which will add to its cost. Slabs and tiles are heavy, hard to manoeuvre and prone to cracking if not handled properly.

Stone is expensive. Its use on any significant scale represents a considerable investment.

Sourcing stone responsibly

Different types of stone are irregularly deposited around the world, which means that stone is often transported quite some distance from where it is mined or quarried to where it is eventually used. Although the energy costs associated with the extraction and processing of stone are not high, comparatively speaking, the costs associated with transportation mean that imported stone cannot be considered an eco-friendly option. At the same time, stone may be a natural material but its supply is not inexhaustible.

• Choose local stone if possible. Fieldstone, or stone cleared from local land, is the archetypal vernacular stone.

• Reclaimed or salvaged stone is another option, particularly if you are considering using a type of stone that is becoming rarer, such as Yorkstone. Sources of salvaged stone include architectural salvage yards, monumental masons (for granite and marble) and demolition sites. Antique stone, reclaimed from country houses and the like, can be very expensive because of its limited supply and unique patina.

Types of stone

There are three main types of stone, the categories corresponding to how and when the stone deposits were first laid down.

• Igneous rocks, such as granite, are the oldest, created thousands of millions of years ago when molten rock cooled and crystallized during the formation of the earth's crust. These rocks are very hard and dense.

• Sedentary rocks, such as limestone and sandstone, date from more recent geological periods. They were formed from deposits laid down on the beds of rivers, lakes and seas and are much softer.

• Metamorphic rocks, such as marble and slate, were formed during the creation of mountain ranges and are the product of intense heat and pressure.

1

2

granite

Smooth, hard and incredibly dense, granite is the toughest natural material in common domestic use. By far the most popular application is as kitchen worktops. Solid granite – for example, the slab form typically used for counters – is more affordable today than it was in the past; tiles, as ever, are cheaper.

The distinctive mottled, granular appearance of the stone is the result of the way in which it was formed, when molten rock cooled and crystallized deep within the earth's crust thousands of millions of years ago. The mineral feldspar is evident in the typical shades of pinks, greys and reds, while mica content shows up in glittery

flecks. Quartz is another mineral that is present in the stone. Found in mountain regions all over the world, granite is principally quarried in Scotland, Devon, Cornwall, Wales, Norway, France, Ireland, eastern Canada and the northeastern United States.

Aesthetically speaking, the material needs plenty of breathing space. Great expanses of granite can be rather dour and relentless, particularly in the darker shades. It is often best used to make a graphic contrast to lighter-toned decoration within a contemporary scheme. Paired with traditional cabinetry and elaborate detailing, the effect can be more banking hall than domestic.

3

Characteristics

• Even, grainy texture with flecked patterning.
• Wide range of beautiful colours including near-black, deep green, reddish brown, blue-grey, pink and gold.
• Hard, dense, heavy and exceptionally wear-resistant, it will not show any appreciable sign of use or wear and tear.
• Thin slabs are prone to

cracking and need careful handling and support.
• Impermeable to water and chemical penetration and resistant to air pollution.
• Granite is more heat-resistant than other types of stone.
• Available as solid slabs; as thinner, lighter tiles in varying dimensions and thicknesses; and in the form of granite setts or paviours – rough-textured blocks.

4

5

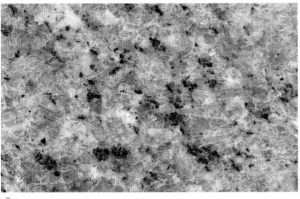

6

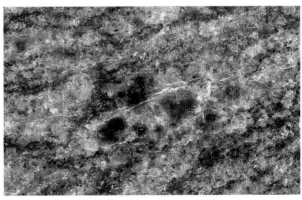

7

Applications

• Granite's resistance to heat, scratch damage, water and stains makes it a practical choice for worktops, kitchen counters, vanity tops and bar tops. Matching edge profiles, splashbacks, door handles, knobs and other types of granite trim are available for a neat and seamless finish. Counters can be supplied pre-cut for sink inserts, with incised drainage grooves.

• Small granite setts can be used to make hardwearing nonslip floors in hallways, garden rooms and other transitional areas, as well as external paving, but they can appear a little municipal.

• Thin granite tiles can be used to clad walls and built-in fixtures such as fireplaces, baths or Jacuzzis. Granite floor tiles are also available; honed finishes are less slippery than highly polished ones.

• Monolithic basins and sinks are also available made of granite.

Finish

• Because granite is so dense, it can be polished to a very high mirror-like gloss, which adds to the natural beauty of the colouring and markings. For a warmer look, choose a matt, honed finish.

• Although granite has low porosity, sealing improves the ease of maintenance.

1. Black granite worktop.
2. Antique brown granite counter with incised drainage grooves.
3.–7. Granite is available in a wide range of strong colours.

1

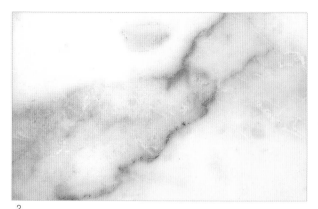

2

3

4

marble

One of the most beautiful of all natural materials and for centuries among the most prized, marble has long been synonymous with luxury and sophistication. In more recent years, however, it might be said to have fallen victim to its own success, with its use at times running the risk of evoking extravagance and ostentation rather than tasteful elegance.

Marble is actually a type of limestone that has been crystallized as a result of the metamorphic transformation of intense heat and pressure. Pure marble is almost completely white. It is the presence of what are technically impurities – minerals such as iron oxides – that gives rise to the wide range of different shades in which marble is obtained. What defines marble more than colour, however, is its milky translucency, which gives it the appearance of softness and depth. This cloudiness is accompanied by other distinctive markings such as cracks, fissures and veining.

The finest-quality marble comes from Italy. Carrara marble, which is pure white, has traditionally been the sculptor's favourite medium.

Characteristics
• Heavy, dense stone that can be polished to a high-gloss finish.
• Available in white, as well as a wide range of colours including russet shades, dull gold, greens and pinks.
• Thin slabs of marble are prone to cracking.
• Marble is not as impervious as granite and must be sealed to promote stain-resistance and ease of maintenance.
• It is traditionally a very expensive form of stone, but new cutting methods have resulted in more economical, lighter, thinner tiles.

Applications
• Marble is traditionally associated with bathroom surfaces – bath surrounds, vanity tops and wall cladding.
• Marble slabs inset into kitchen counters are ideal pastry-making surfaces. Marble is not stain-resistant enough to make a practical worktop.
• Wall and floor tiles are cheaper than solid slabs and

5

come in a range of dimensions. Edge profiles and other forms of marble trim are also available.
• Marble is frequently used in fire surrounds, both as mantel shelves and facing stones.
• Simple marble basins, pedestal sinks and baths in pure geometric forms have a timeless quality.

Finish
• Highly polished mirror finishes make marble very slippery and are best reserved for wall tiles, counters and cladding.
• Floor tiles may be honed for better grip underfoot.
• Marble can also be subtly aged by 'tumbling', a process that removes the sharp edges and smooth face of the stone to create a more rustic and slip-resistant surface.
• Marble requires sealing to prevent dirt and stains from penetrating the surface.

1. Marble-clad bathroom.
2.–4. Marble colourways.
5. The ultimate in luxury – smooth, pure white marble used as a bathroom finish.

1

2

3

slate

A metamorphic rock like marble, slate is what results when shale, a fine-grained rock composed of silt and clay, is exposed to tremendous heat and pressure. The high mica content of slate and the way in which this was transformed during the metamorphic process mean that slate can easily be split or riven into thin planes. This quality, in turn, makes it an incredibly versatile stone for use in construction and finishing, whether as roofing slates or tiles, cladding or paving.

Good sources of slate include Wales, Devon, Cornwall (for bluestone, a slate from Delabole) and various regions in North America, South America, India, Spain and Africa.

Characteristics

- Hard, wear-resistant and waterproof.
- Easily split into thin planes for use as roofing slates or tiles. Laterally strong, which means that thin planes or tiles will not crack readily, unlike other types of stone.
- Sleek, 'wet-look' texture due to the mica content.
- Available in a range of dark, moody colours, including blue-black, dull purple and grey-green. Indian, Mexican and African slate is brighter and more colourful. Mottled patterning.
- Available in a wide range of formats, including tiles and slabs of varying dimensions. Riven or split slabs are thicker and smaller than sawn slate.

Applications

- Huge range of applications, including roofing, cladding, tiling, flooring, shelving and countertops.

Finish

- Seal before and after grouting.

1. Horizontal slate tiles cladding an exterior wall.
2. Slate flooring in a kitchen.
3. Riven texture.
4. White grouting makes a graphic contrast to dark slate flooring.
5. Slate is available in strong colours.
6.–9. A range of slate tones and textures.

4

5

6

7

8

9

1

2

travertine

Although travertine is sometimes referred to as a limestone and sometimes as a marble, it is neither. In fact, travertine is a sedimentary stone that is composed of layers of calcite deposited by organic matter in hot springs and spas. Fossilized traces of leaves, feathers and branches are often seen in the stone.

For centuries, travertine's hardness and beauty has meant that it has been prized as a construction material. The most famous source is Tivoli, near Rome, and the largest building made of travertine is the Colosseum.

Characteristics
• Travertine has a honeycomb structure, the result of water bubbling through the deposits prior to crystallization. This is revealed in the form of small holes or pits on the surface of the cut stone.
• Very strong stone, despite its pitted appearance.
• The purest travertine is white; colours (warm grey through to coral red) are the result of impurities, such as minerals.
• Available in tiles, slabs and cladding panels.

Applications
• Favoured by modern architects as a façade or cladding material.
• Tiles and slabs can be used for flooring indoors and out. Travertine is a popular paving material for patios and paths.
• Travertine panels make

3

elegant wall cladding.
• Bathroom sinks made of travertine are also available.

Finish
• Travertine is hard enough to take a high polish, but honed surfaces are preferable if the material is to be used as flooring.
• Surface holes may be left unfilled for a natural texture or filled in the factory with hard resin and honed smooth.
• Travertine requires sealing to promote stain- and dirt-resistance.

1. Travertine wall tiles with matching moulding.
2. Travertine flooring.
3. A pitted texture is typical.

2

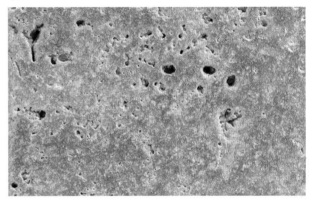

3

limestone

Limestone is the term for a group of sedimentary rocks composed of layers of calcium carbonate, either the residue of organic matter, such as sea creatures, corals and plants laid down by rivers and seas, or carbonates deposited through precipitation. These strata were then turned to stone by millions of years of pressure.

Different types of limestone vary significantly in appearance and characteristics. Although, like all sedimentary stones, limestone is softer and more porous than igneous rocks, a few types approach the hardness of granite.

Limestone is quarried all over the world. French limestone, however, is considered among the finest, being harder and less porous than other types. Caen stone, quarried around Boulogne, is a chalky colour. In Britain limestone deposits are found in a curving band that begins at Portland Bill in Dorset, continues through the Cotswolds and up to the Humber and Cleveland Hills of Yorkshire. English limestone includes Bath or Cotswold stone (a warm golden colour), the stone used to construct Oxford colleges, and Portland stone (milky white), from which many public buildings in London were constructed. Indiana limestone is a notable North American type; other well-known sources include Italy, Israel and Portugal.

Characteristics

• Typically pale and cool in tone, in neutral shades ranging from off-white to pale gold to grey. More intense colours are also found, including a particularly vibrant blue – an unusual stone colour.

• Textured surface patterned with flecks, veins or mottling. Fossilized traces of animal or vegetable life are common.

• Tends to be softer and more porous than igneous stones such as granite. Some types, however, are harder and denser.

• Widely available in slabs, tiles and panels for wall cladding.

Applications

• Because of its porosity and hence its tendency to stain, limestone is not commonly used for countertops.

• Limestone makes an elegant contemporary floor, the perfect backdrop for pared-down modern interiors.

• Basins are also available.

Finish

• Limestone won't take a high-gloss polish. The standard finish, by sandblasting or honing, creates a matt surface with a degree of friction to prevent slipping; honing intensifies the colour.

• Limestone must be sealed (and the seal repeated at regular intervals) to protect against staining.

1. Cool limestone flooring.
2.–3. Range of limestone tones.

sandstone

A sedimentary rock, sandstone is composed of sand grains cemented together under pressure. Its high quartz content makes it considerably harder than limestone.

One of the most famous types of sandstone is Yorkstone. Quarried in Yorkshire, and becoming increasingly rare owing to its long-term popularity, Yorkstone has been particularly sought-after as an outdoor paving material, since it is hard, frostproof and can be split or riven to give a nonslip surface.

Characteristics
• Harder and denser than other types of sedimentary stone, such as limestone.
• Granular texture. Colours are sandy shades of pale brown to reddish brown. Yorkstone is greyish brown.
• Available in flags, setts, cobbles, small blocks and tiles.

Applications
• Chiefly used as flooring. Rustic-looking Yorkstone is popular as external paving.

Finish
• Sandblasted or honed finishes. Yorkstone is usually riven for a ridged nonslip surface.
• For indoor applications, sandstone must be sealed.

1. Warm sandstone flooring and steps.
2. Sandstone makes an understated floor.
3. Smooth sandstone flooring contrasting with a rugged stone fireplace.

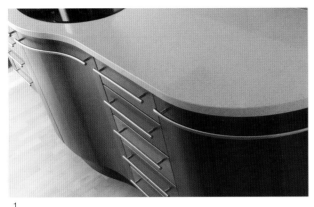

1

2

3

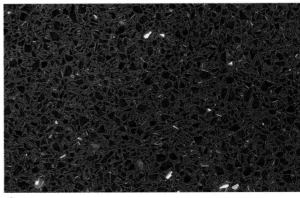

4

engineered stone

Manufacturers of artificial stone seek to replicate the beauty of the natural material while delivering certain practical benefits, not least reduced cost. Some of these products, particularly those that are composed of a high proportion of natural stone, are very convincing; others less so.

Processes vary, but many types of engineered stone entail combining and compacting some proportion of natural stone (often quartz, which is readily available) with polyester resins and pigments. The result – in slab, counter or tile format – is generally maintenance-free, stain-resistant, antibacterial and consistent in colour and pattern. Some types of engineered stone are stronger than the real thing.

One type of product has been designed for ease of installation. This material, which blends granite with polymers in a high-tech process, can be fitted directly to the top of existing counters, vanity units, splashbacks and other surfaces. It is nonporous and heat-resistant up to 149°C. Each top is custom-made to individual specification.

1. Kitchen counter in engineered stone.
2.–6. Engineered stone is available in a wide variety of vivid colours.

5

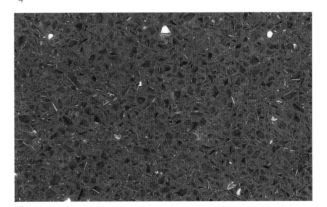

6

function, format & maintenance

As a natural material, stone is not consistent across the board. Colours and surface patterning will vary, even in stone worked from the same quarry. Before installation, it is important to make sure that the tiles or slabs are as evenly matched as possible; suppliers should be able to assist. Installers can also make on-the-spot adjustments to blend colours as harmoniously as possible.

Wastage

Always make allowances for wastage when ordering stone. Even the most experienced installer will not be able to prevent a certain amount of wastage through damage in transit or cracking in situ.

Flooring

• Formats for flooring include slabs (riven or sawn), flags, setts, cobbles and tiles. Tiles range from 1cm to 2cm thick. In larger dimensions tiles must be thicker to resist cracking.
• Floors can be laid in a number of different patterns – for example, staggered courses, chequerboard or in the form of irregular flagstones. A classic pattern combines light-coloured octagons (marble or limestone) with dark cabuchon insets (slate).
• The subfloor must be strong enough to take the weight, which may rule out timber floors on upper levels in the case of heavier, thicker slabs. The subfloor must also be perfectly even, flat and inflexible, as any movement will cause the stone to crack.

Two layers of boarding may be required for timber subfloors.
• Installation is either by embedding in sand and cement or by gluing in place. Most stone tiles are laid on a bed of proprietary adhesive to the thickness recommended by the manufacturer.
• Stone flooring of any reasonable expanse must incorporate movement joints (up to 1cm wide) around the perimeter to allow for changes caused by variations in temperature, humidity or any flexing of the subfloor.
• Regular tiles can be laid butted up closely together. Hand-finished, riven or overtly textured slabs or tiles need wider joints. Choose grouting to match the stone colour.

Cladding

• Wall tiles may be as thin as 6mm.
• Tiles up to about 1.5cm thick can be glued in place; any thicker and they will need to be anchored using special steel fixings.

Worksurfaces

• For counters, hearths, fire surrounds, vanity tops and other built-in surfaces, stone is generally available in slabs between 2.5cm and 5cm thick.
• The size of the slab is a function of the stone type. Slabs of a larger dimension are preferable for covering greater areas, as there will not be the need for so many joints.
• Stone can be cut, contoured and incised (with drainage grooves), according to specification.

• The supporting framework must be robust enough to take the weight, even and inflexible.
• Worksurfaces are installed by gluing with proprietary adhesive.

Sinks and baths

• Stone sinks and baths are available in a number of simple forms, including troughs, tanks, hemispheres and the like.
• Weight is an issue. Check that the bathroom's subfloor can take the additional load; otherwise, the existing floor structure may need to be strengthened.

Maintenance

Stone appears to be so strong and immutable that it may be tempting to view it as a maintenance-free material. This is far from the case. All stone, even granite, should be sealed to prevent a build-up of dirt and grime and the seal should be renewed at regular intervals. Most worktops are supplied ready-sealed.
• Stone should be sealed both before and after grouting; sometimes before and after gluing. This is necessary to prevent any discolouration and staining during installation.
• Floors: For general maintenance, mop frequently using a dry nontreated dust mop. Grit does the most damage, so provide doormats or rugs outside the entrance to trap loose dirt and prevent it from being tracked over the floor. Dirty patches can be scrubbed with water and a neutral detergent, but avoid wet mopping.
• Counters: Clean with neutral

cleanser, stone soap or mild washing-up liquid and water. Avoid overwetting or using too much detergent. Rinse and dry.
• Acids such as cola, lemon juice, wine and vinegar are extremely harmful to stone. Tackle spills immediately.
• Don't use oils or wax polishes on stone.

Opposite: Properly maintained, stone should last for generations.

brick & ceramic

Made from clay, one of the most basic of all natural ingredients, brick and other ceramic products have an intrinsic earthiness, warmth and domestic quality. Scaled to fit the human hand, they contribute an inherent rhythm to surfaces and finishes that comes from the repetitive nature of the grid or courses in which they are laid. Depending on glazing or surface texture, they can be simple and robust, traditional or contemporary, luminous and shimmering or rough and rustic.

Although not as massive, as a construction material, brick has similar thermal properties to stone in that it absorbs heat slowly and releases it slowly, which makes it an asset in buildings designed around passive solar-gain strategies. Brick is the oldest man-made building material – bricks made of earth mixed with straw and baked in the sun represent construction technology at its very simplest. A standard house-building material in northern Europe for centuries, it has also played a role in more modernist designs, with expanses of exposed brickwork being one of the defining features of the contemporary loft interior.

Ceramic tiles, from the traditional terracotta or 'fired earth' floor tile to richly glazed tiles made from refined clay, are immensely varied stylistically. They remain one of the most popular means of covering floors and walls, particularly in kitchens and bathrooms where practical issues are at the forefront. Glazed tiles are water- and stain-resistant; all ceramic tiles are hardwearing.

In the nineteenth century, industrialization introduced regularity to what had formerly been handmade products displaying local variation of material, decorative style and technique. While most bricks and ceramic tiles are mass-produced today, there has been a revival of interest in handmade terracotta tiles, in particular. Mosaic has also enjoyed a recent surge of popularity that shows no signs of abating.

Practicalities

• Brick and ceramic are by and large relatively inexpensive and widely available.

• Bricklaying aside, these materials require only a modest degree of skill to install. An out-and-out amateur may bodge or bungle a tiling job, but it is generally within the scope of those experienced in DIY techniques.

• The most successful uses of these earthen materials depend on wholehearted application and attention to pattern and scale. Skimpy areas of tiling – narrow splashbacks, for example – are simply dreary; fully tiled walls are not, even when the tile is plain and utilitarian.

• Larger tiles suit larger areas; small tiles are best where space is more limited.

Opposite: Exposed brick lends warmth and depth of character.

1

2

3

4

brick

Before industrialization, all bricks were handmade from local deposits of clay and fired in wood- or coal-fuelled kilns. The result was naturally lively and varied, characteristics still evident in domestic brick buildings dating from before the nineteenth century. You can still get handmade bricks today, but they are very expensive.

Types of brick
• **Standard construction bricks**
Available in different grades and a range of colours from salmon pink to purplish brown. London stock bricks are yellow when new, mellowing to grey-brown.
• **Lightweight bricks**
Honeycombed with air pockets, these have greater insulation properties.

• **Weathered bricks**
The distressed 'tumbled' appearance suggests wear.
• **Waterstruck bricks** These have an overt raised texture.
• **Wirecut bricks** These bricks are extruded from moulds and cut by wire for crisp outlines.
• **Engineering bricks** Made from unrefined clay, pressed and burnt. Suitable for external use and as outdoor paving, they are resistant to wear, frost, chemicals and impact.
• **Brick paviours** Made from refined clay and fired at high temperatures, these are thinner than standard bricks. They are very durable, waterproof and are available with nonslip textures.
• **Second-hand or salvaged bricks** These can be more expensive than new bricks.

Characteristics
• Warm earthen colours and matt texture.
• Heavy material when laid. Good thermal mass, ideal for passive solar-heating strategies or for use over underfloor heating.
• High embodied energy because of the heat required for firing; energy costs also associated with transportation.
• Readily available and relatively inexpensive.
• Standard bricks are porous and stain readily.
• Patterns can be created depending on the way bricks are laid – traditional designs include herringbone, stretcher bond and basketweave.
• Bricklaying is a job for a professional.

Applications
• To form load-bearing walls in masonry construction.
• Internal walls, partitions and fireplace surrounds. Exposed brickwork makes a warm backdrop to rustic or contemporary interiors.
• Flooring. Bricks must be laid over a solid concrete subfloor in a sand and cement bed. A damp-proof membrane may be required between the bricks and the mortar bed. Joints should be grouted immediately. Movement joints through the floor and around the perimeter, filled with elastic sealant, allow for subsequent movement through changes in humidity.
• Only nonporous fully vitrified bricks should be used as outdoor paving.

5

6

7

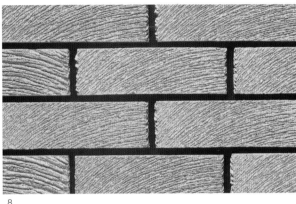

8

9

10

Finish

• Although standard bricks are porous, sealing is not advised. Interior brick walls need occasional dusting.

• Nonporous paviours can be lightly dressed with linseed oil or similar to resist dirt.

• Generally maintenance-free. Newly laid bricks may show 'efflorescence' or deposits of white mineral salts on the surface. This is remedied by washing with water.

• Brickwork can be painted indoors and out. This treatment preserves the natural rhythm of the surface while broadening the colour possibilities.

1.–10. Brick is widely available in a range of textures and earthy colours.

Overleaf:
11. Original brick walls can be sandblasted to remove previous finishes.
12. The contrasting textures of brick, wood and glass bring a dynamic quality to a scheme.

WORTH TRYING, Mornington Crescent lift, 30.06, 5:45ish You smiled at me, I smiled at you. You were getting out of the lift and I in.

11

1

2

3

terracotta tiles

Like bricks, terracotta tiles are earthen products that have been made for centuries in parts of the world where there are clay deposits. They can be glazed or unglazed, handmade or manufactured, antique or new. In recent years there has been a particular revival of interest in handmade terracotta tiles, which display characterful variations and irregularities as a result of differences in the raw material and the way in which it is shaped and fired.

Types of terracotta tile
• **Handmade unglazed tiles** New tiles made in the traditional manner are available from a variety of sources, including Provence and Mexico. Tiles are generally shaped by hand,

baked in the sun and then fired in a wood-burning kiln. Typical colours include yellow (Bordeaux), pale pink (Provence), deep red (Burgundy), ochre (Tuscany) and orange (Mexico). The surface of the tile may show flame marks or shading where clays are blended.
• **Machine-made unglazed tiles** These have a finer surface texture than handmade tiles and a regular shape; they are also available with a distressed finish. Computer techniques may be used to produce the type of variety in colour from tile to tile that is characteristic of handmade tiles.
• **Glazed tiles** Available in a range of colours, patterns and textures. Handmade and mass-produced tiles may be glazed.

• **Antique pammets** Traditional terracotta tiles (generally 10in square) reclaimed from barns, manor houses, farm houses and chateaux. These are very pricey.

Characteristics
• Absorb and release heat slowly. Terracotta tiles can be used over underfloor heating.
• Leathery patina deepens with age and use.
• Durable. Glazed terracotta tiles, however, are not as durable as glazed ceramic tiles.
• The format is generally square, but rectangles and octagons are also available.

Applications
• Unglazed terracotta tiles are exclusively used for floors. Handmade tiles, which are

uneven in thickness, are best laid by a professional. The subfloor should be dry, even and rigid. Tiles are laid in a mortar bed or glued with proprietary adhesive and then grouted.
• Glazed terracotta tiles are not durable enough to be used on the floor, but they make good wall cladding. Some varieties are too porous for kitchen worktops and shower enclosures.

Finish
• Unglazed tiles are porous and require sealing with linseed oil or wax. Some tiles are ready-sealed by the manufacturer. Sweep regularly to prevent grit from damaging the surface.
• Glazed tiles are still liable to staining from acidic liquids or foods. Avoid strong detergents.

4

quarry tiles

Utilitarian and mass-produced, quarry tiles are a cheap and practical alternative to terracotta tiles. They are made from unrefined high-silica clay pressed into a mould and then burnt.

Characteristics

• Heavy, durable and wear-resistant. Can be used over underfloor heating, as they absorb and lose heat slowly.

• Available in a limited range of clay colours – red, brown, biscuit and black. Rough texture and square format.
• Cheap.
• Rather static, lifeless quality when compared to terracotta tiles. They do not change appreciably with use.

Applications

• Flooring, particularly in utility areas, kitchens, halls, garden rooms and similar locations.

Finish

Nonporous quarry tiles may be lightly dressed with linseed oil or wax.

1. Handmade terracotta tiles have almost a leathery look.
2.–3. Colours may vary from ochre and pink to deep red.
4. Quarry tiles are uniform and regular. They tend to suit country locations better than urban ones.

1

2

ceramic tiles

Ceramic tiles are mass-produced clay products that are available in a huge range of colours, textures and patterns, as well as a number of different shapes and sizes. The chief distinction within the category is between nonporcelain ceramic tiles and porcelain tiles, with the latter being stronger, more durable and more expensive. Both types of ceramic tile are made from clay and fired in a kiln. Porcelain tiles, however, contain other minerals, notably feldspar, which contribute to their hardness, and are fired at higher temperatures. While most nonporcelain tiles are finished with a glaze, porcelain tiles can be glazed, unglazed or 'full body', where the colour runs through the tile.

Another variation on the theme are encaustic tiles, which are through-patterned. Instead of the design or colour being applied to the top of the tile in the form of a glaze or textural embossing, it is inlaid in different colours of clays. Encaustic tiles are generally used as feature or inset tiles within a plain tiled surface.

Characteristics

• Regularity – tiles are uniform, which means that they can be laid in precise grids and at narrow spacings. Most common formats are 10cm and 15cm square. Rectangular 'metro' tiles with bevelled edges have a retro quality.
• All ceramic tiles are durable, but some are more durable

than others. Porcelain tiles are the hardest – 30 per cent harder than granite – and are less likely to break and chip.
• Ceramic tiles are water- and stain-resistant. Again, porcelain tiles perform better in this capacity, too.
• Widely available. Some of the highest-quality (and most expensive) tiles come from Italy. Porcelain tiles are more expensive than standard ceramic.
• Can be cold, slippery and ungiving underfoot.
• Huge range of colours, textures and patterns, enabling you to coordinate tiling with any style or decorative scheme. Dados, beadings and other forms of matching trim are also available.

Applications

• Whatever the application, if you are inexperienced at tiling or DIY generally, it is probably best to employ a professional for the installation. Expect a degree of wastage, both in transit and during tiling – 10 per cent is not uncommon. Broken or chipped tiles can be used when cuts need to be made around obstacles.
• **Flooring** Choose a tile with the relevant degree of durability for the location. Some tiles are harder than others and are capable of withstanding heavy traffic; others suit only light wear applications, such as bathroom floors. The subfloor needs to be dry, even and inflexible. It is often a good idea, particularly if you are

3

4

5

6

7

creating a pattern or complex design, to dry-lay the tiles first so you can come up with a layout that minimizes cutting. Tiles are generally glued in place with a proprietary adhesive and then grouted. If you are tiling a large expanse of floor, movement joints around the perimeter, or through the tiling at intervals, are advisable.

• **Wall cladding** Tiling is particularly effective if it is used wholeheartedly, rather than simply around the margins of sinks, baths and so on. If you want to stop the tiling short of the ceiling, align the top edge with an existing feature, such as the top or bottom of a window. The underlying surface must be dry and even. Use waterproof adhesive in wet areas and heatproof adhesive behind stoves and hobs.

• **Worksurfaces** The more stain- and water-resistant types of tile can be used to make countertops. These tiles are generally thicker than wall tiles and are fully vitrified to withstand heat.

Finish

• Glazed ceramic tiles need no subsequent finishing.
• Stained or dirty grout can be cleaned with mild detergent and a stiff brush.

1. Classic blue and white ceramic tiles.
2. Glazed ceramic tiles in a rectangular 'metro' format.
3. Rectangular blue tiles laid in staggered rows.
4. Glazed ceramic tile.
5. Encaustic tile.
6.–7. Encaustic tile featuring Moorish designs.

2

3

mosaic

The smallest tiles of all are mosaic tesserae. Although included in this section because it shares a format and types of application with other clay tiles, mosaic is not exclusively a ceramic product. Mosaic can also be made of stone, glass and glass-and-resin mixtures (see pages 162–3).

Mosaic is an ancient art that dates back thousands of years. It has seen a recent revival of interest, both as a means of decorating walls and floors with complex patterns and imagery, and as a clean-lined backdrop for showers, wet rooms and bathrooms. Mosaic picture-making demands considerable artistry; one-off commissions for a decorative feature are generally fairly expensive.

Characteristics

• Mosaic surfaces 'read' in two ways – up close with a crispness of detail, and at a distance with a soft, luminous delicacy.
• Ceramic and glass mosaic (tesserae) are evenly dimensioned and easier to lay than stone mosaic.
• Huge range of vivid colours as well as natural 'stone' shades.
• Widely available in sheet form, with a backing of netting or peel-off paper, to make tiling simpler and quicker. Sheets may be single colour or a random selection of colours.
• Grouting gives mosaic surfaces a key, since there is proportionally more of it per tile than in the case of larger tile formats. The colour of the grouting should be chosen

with care – light-coloured grout for light-toned tiles, and so on, will create a seamless effect, while a contrasting grout brings out a more graphic quality.

Applications

• **Flooring** The requirements for the subfloor are the same as for ceramic tiles. Also like ceramic tiles, mosaic sheets are laid using proprietary adhesive and grouted once they have cured. Choose honed stone mosaic rather than polished and ceramic, rather than glass, for flooring applications.
• **Wall cladding** Mosaic is the only type of tiling that can cover curved sections of wall effectively.
• For more complex patterns or images, mosaic can be laid in one of two ways. The first,

which is incredibly labour-intensive, is to piece the design together tile by tile. The second is to make your own mosaic sheets by sticking individual tiles face down on paper with water-soluble glue, grouting the backs of the tiles and sticking the sheet in place. Once all the sections are laid, the paper is wetted and peeled off before final grouting.

Finish

• Do not polish mosaic flooring or it will be too slippery.
• Washing with a mild detergent is generally sufficient for ordinary maintenance.

1. Mosaic-tiled fireplace.
2. Pearlized mosaic.
3. White stone mosaic.
Opposite: Metallic mosaic used to clad a bathroom wall.

linoleum

Go back a couple of generations and you would have been hard pressed to find anyone prepared to award linoleum the status of a classic material. It was a make-do product, brittle and unlovely, the flooring of pre-war kitchens and hospital corridors. Lino was second best, a stand-in for hard tiles or other types of flooring that were more expensive, and was often patterned in simulation of those surfaces.

Yet several decades ago, lino's dreary image had a dramatic makeover. Changes in the manufacturing process resulted in a product that was much improved in both practical and aesthetic terms. A wide range of colours and patterns became available for the first time and the material itself was less prone to cracking, which was a particular failure of earlier lino.

Because old-style linoleum was generally produced in patterns that aped other materials, it was widely assumed that lino was itself a synthetic. In fact, it is an entirely natural

1

2

3

4

product, whose name derives from oleum lini or linseed oil, one of its principal ingredients. Today lino's environmental credentials recommend it to those for whom ecological issues, as well as health and wellbeing, are high up on the agenda.

The basic process and recipe was devised in 1863 by Frederick Walton. Aside from linseed oil, other ingredients of linoleum include hessian or jute, which are used for backing, pine resin, powdered cork, wood flour, powdered limestone and pigment. The mixture is pressed onto the backing, left to dry for a period of weeks and then baked at a high temperature.

1.–4. Lino is available in a wide range of soft colours. A mottled patterning is typical.
5. Yellow and white lino-tiled floor.

5

Characteristics

- Lino is smooth with a slightly granular appearance. The finish is naturally matt.
- The colour range is very wide, widest in sheet lino, though colours are softer and less intense than those of synthetic materials.
- Textural effects include mottled, marbled or flecked surfaces.
- Patterns are also available, including geometrics such as plaids, stripes and tumbling blocks.
- Warm and resilient underfoot, it provides a comfortable, relatively nonslip surface.
- Water-resistant. However, lino can be damaged by damp penetrating the joins.
- Antibacterial, which is why lino has long been used as a flooring in hospitals, clinics, schools and other spaces where hygiene is very important.
- Antistatic and hypoallergenic. Lino is a good flooring material if there is an asthma-sufferer in the household, as it repels dust mites, which are a significant trigger for asthmatic attacks.
- Resistant to burns and chemical damage.
- Lino matures as it ages and actually becomes harder with time.
- Available in sheet or tile formats. The best-quality lino is thick, strong and flexible.

Applications

Lino's chief application is as flooring. While it is most commonly used in kitchens, bathrooms and playrooms, lino can make a glossy and stylish covering for living areas, too, especially in solid colours or in neutral shades such as white or grey.

- The subfloor must be perfectly smooth, even and dry. This may entail covering existing floorboards with a layer of hardboard to prevent ridges showing through the material and causing patches of wear.
- Before laying, lino must be brought into the area where it will be installed and allowed to acclimatize to existing temperature and humidity conditions for a period of up to 48 hours.
- The easiest format to manage is tiles. These are lighter and more readily manipulated than sheet flooring and installation can be carried out by a competent amateur. Tiles are stuck down using a proprietary adhesive and butted up tightly so that water does not penetrate the joins. Damaged tiles can be lifted and replaced individually.
- Sheet lino gives a smooth surface, which is relatively

seamless depending on the floor area. However, it is very heavy and unwieldy, and laying requires special equipment, which makes installation a professional job. The seams must be heat-welded and the lino rolled to ensure it is perfectly flat.

- Patterns can be created very simply by alternating colours to produce a chequerboard effect or by framing an expanse of solid-colour lino with a contrasting border. More complex inlaid designs, including one-off commissions, may be created by computer-controlled cutting with high-pressure water jets.

Finish

- A temporary discolouration may show up after laying in certain shades of lino, especially in lino that is white, grey or blue. This is a yellow tint known as 'stove yellowing'. It disappears after the lino has been exposed to daylight – in a few hours if the area receives good natural light, longer if it is in a semi-basement or basement location.
- Lino does not require sealing. To give it a glossy sheen, you can apply emulsion polish, but avoid overpolishing in areas where you are likely to slip.
- Regular maintenance consists of dusting or vacuuming to remove loose grit. You can also wash the surface using a damp mop and mild detergent, but avoid overwetting the floor.
- Lino is resistant to many chemicals. Permanent damage, however, can be caused by solvents, washing soda and oven cleaner.
- As lino is through-coloured, cigarette burns can be rubbed away.

1. Vibrant lino flooring in a boy's bedroom.
2. Lino is quiet, hygienic and comfortable underfoot.
3. Lino is easy to maintain and improves with age.
4. Muted grey sheet lino makes an unobtrusive floor covering.

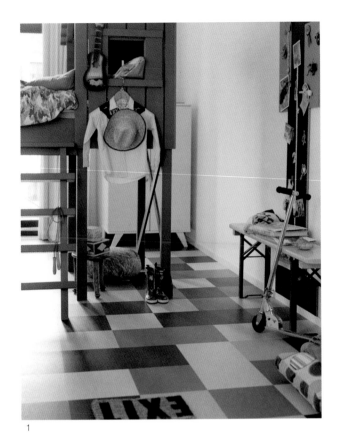

1

2

3

4

vinyl

Unlike linoleum, vinyl is wholly synthetic. The basic ingredient is PVC or polyvinylchloride, a thermoplastic first developed in the 1950s. This family of plastics, which includes polythene and polystyrene, can be formed into complex shapes and retains the ability to be softened by heat, which gives flexibility.

Vinyl is present in our homes in many diverse forms, but usually as flooring. Vinyl tiles or sheet are common, economic and practical coverings for utility areas such as kitchens, bathrooms and laundry rooms. Other uses include as shower curtains, table coverings and inflatable furniture, as well as behind-the-scenes applications such as damp-proof membranes and window frames.

The environmental costs associated with the manufacture of any plastic, the difficulties associated with disposal and possible concerns about the chemical composition of PVC in relation to human health mean that the use of vinyl is discouraged by the green lobby. However, good-quality vinyl has the potential to last

1

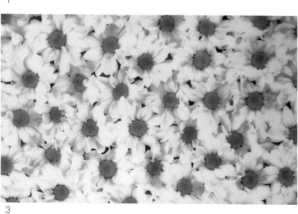

2

3

4

several decades, which means it should not necessarily be viewed as a disposable material. Good-quality vinyl generally comes with a lifetime warranty on manufacturing defects and wear.

This section deals primarily with vinyl's use as a floor covering. Like linoleum, vinyl floors come in two basic formats – as tiles and as sheets (2m, 3m and 4m wide). Both tiles and sheets are composed of several layers: a backing (the thickness of which determines durability), a printed design layer, a clear film that protects against rips and gouges, and a protective top layer that enhances maintenance. In the case of vinyl sheet, the backing may either be felt or fibreglass.

1. Wood-effect vinyl.
2. Wood-effect vinyl flooring.
3. Vinyl-covered cork-backed tile in a daisy pattern.
4. Vinyl-covered cork-backed tile in a pebbles pattern.
5. Vinyl with a woven design.
6. Blue-grey flecked pattern.
7. Vinyl-covered cork-backed tile in a bubbles pattern.
8. Vinyl-covered cork-backed tile in a cork pattern.

5

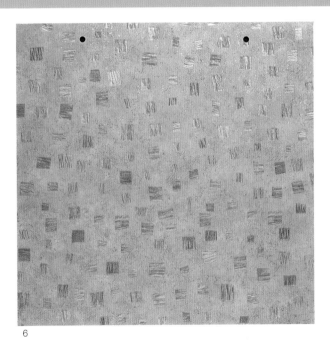

6

7

8

Characteristics

- There is a vast array of colours, textures and patterns on the market, which makes for broad stylistic choice. Colours range from bright, intense shades to more subtle natural-looking tones. Patterns can be bold and graphic or more traditional in style.
- Modern print and embossing techniques mean that contemporary vinyl can simulate the appearance and texture of natural materials such as wood, stone, slate and ceramic very effectively.
- Vinyl designed for retail or commercial use may incorporate flecks of quartz to increase slip-resistance.
- The thicker grades perform better and are more comfortable and resilient underfoot. Cushioned vinyl is particularly kind to feet and knees, and objects are less likely to break when dropped.
- In comparison with most natural materials, vinyl is very economic and is widely available from mass-market outlets.
- Vinyl is water-resistant, which makes it suitable for utility areas such as kitchens, bathrooms and laundry rooms, and for households that include children or pets. It is also practical in areas of heavy traffic, though it is unsuitable for use on stairs.
- The better, thicker grades are resistant to scratches, stains, fading and ripping, as well as household chemicals and grease.
- Vinyl will not increase a home's value, unlike a natural floor covering such as hardwood or stone. It does not improve with wear and use, but merely looks shoddy.
- It is not considered environmentally friendly, as petroleum and natural gas are used in its manufacture. It has also been identified as one of those materials that 'offgas', or release potentially harmful chemicals into the atmosphere, and as such can compromise indoor air quality. If vinyl catches fire, the fumes are toxic.

Applications

Vinyl's most common application is as flooring, particularly in utility areas or areas of heavy traffic. Installation of vinyl varies according to whether you are laying tiles or sheet, and according to the type of backing. Sheet vinyl in the larger widths enable you to cover an average-sized room seamlessly.

- All vinyl must be laid over a dry, even subfloor. You can lay vinyl over concrete, wood, plywood or hardboard. Any irregularities in the underlying surface will show up in the final floor and create wear patches.
- Vinyl tiles are much easier to install than vinyl sheet, as

they are lighter and easier to manipulate. Some can be lifted and repositioned, which means that you do not have to be so precise in preparation. Glueless tiles are sold with an underlayer that simplifies placement and come with tabs or spray adhesive. Other tiles may have a peel-off layer, so that they can be stuck in place. The highest-quality vinyl tiles should be stuck down with a proprietary adhesive.
- Vinyl sheet requires careful cutting to size and can be heavy and awkward to work with. Installation is possible for a competent amateur, but professional assistance may be preferable. Sheet with felt backing is laid over trowelled-on adhesive, either over the entire surface or around the perimeter. Sheet with fibreglass backing can be laid loose, laid over spot adhesive or laid over a full adhesive application. The latter is more durable but harder to remove. Loose-laid fibreglass-backed vinyl requires a movement joint around the perimeter to cope with variations in temperature and humidity that might affect the subfloor.
- While vinyl is water-resistant, the adhesive is not, and moisture penetration along seams is an issue. Tiles are more prone to water damage than sheets because of the increased number of seams and joints.

Finish

- Vinyl is resistant to water and many chemicals. However, cleaning products containing bleach can stain, as can rubber heels.
- Standing water can penetrate seams, lift tiles and cause damage to the subfloor, so spills must be mopped up promptly.
- Cigarette burns cause permanent damage, as the material is highly flammable.
- Aside from the above, vinyl is virtually maintenance-free and needs no sealing, polishing or waxing. Simple dusting and damp mopping are sufficient for routine care.

Opposite: Classic black and white vinyl flooring makes a fresh and practical surface.

carpet

Although carpet may lack the ultra-luxurious connotations it once had in the days when wall-to-wall carpeting was the last word in interior fashion, it remains consistently popular, especially for areas in the home where a softer surface is welcome underfoot, such as bedrooms. Carpet positively invites contact and if you like to wander around the house in bare feet, sit or lounge on the floor, or have young children at the crawling and toddling stage, carpet will provide you with the extra dimension of warmth and easy comfort that you require.

Fitted or wall-to-wall carpet is an undoubted space-enhancer, particularly in open-plan layouts or in homes that are arranged on one level. By contrast, carpeting can also be used to signal the shift between more public areas of the home and intimate private retreats, and thus help to create a sense of enclosure.

Carpeting varies widely in fibre content, pile construction and density, with an equivalent variation in terms of quality and price. It is always a good idea to buy the best you can afford: cheap carpet wears incredibly badly and will need replacing sooner rather than later.

Opposite: Carpeted areas or rugs can be used for spatial definition, to anchor a dining area, for example, within an open-plan space.

Characteristics

- Warm, comfortable and resilient.
- Insulates against impact sound and is suitable for use on stairs.
- Carpet rots when exposed to damp and is not suitable for family bathrooms, kitchens or utility areas.
- Blends are more hardwearing than all-wool carpets.
- Widely available in a huge range of colours, patterns and textures, and in a variety of pile types.
- Carpet comes in different grades to suit different locations and degrees of wear.
- Carpet widths vary. Anything greater than 1.8m is known as broadloom.
- According to composition and surface treatment, carpet varies in stain-resistance. In general, it requires greater vigilance than other materials to remain in good condition.
- Fitted carpet can harbour dust mites, pet hair and flea eggs. It is inadvisable to choose carpet if there is an allergy-sufferer in the household.
- Only all-wool or all-natural-fibre carpets are eco friendly.

Types of carpet construction

Until the 1950s, all carpets were woven. New manufacturing techniques introduced tufted carpets, which are generally cheaper than woven though not necessarily of lower quality.

- **Woven carpets** The pile is woven along with the backing. Strong, hardwearing and fairly expensive. Styles of woven carpet include Axminster (typically featuring many colours), Wilton (often smooth, cut pile) and flatweave, which have no pile.
- **Tufted carpets** The pile is inserted into the backing, which is coated with adhesive to keep the pile in place. The pile may be left in loops, cut or a combination of the two. A secondary backing may be added to give strength. Most tufted carpets are solid colours.
- **Nonwoven carpets** Cheap, mass-produced carpets and carpet tiles. Fibres are glued, flocked or needle-punched to the backing. No pile.

Density

The ability of carpet to withstand wear is a function of its density, or how closely the fibres are packed together, and not the thickness or depth of the pile. If you press the pile down with your thumb and it recovers quickly, this is a good indication that the carpet is dense. Pile weights are generally given on the carpet label:

• Light domestic use, for example bedrooms: up to 800g per square metre.
• Light to medium domestic use, for example living rooms: 875g per square metre.
• Medium to heavy domestic use, for example family rooms: 950g per square metre.
• Heavy domestic use, for example halls and stairs: 1kg per square metre.

Types of fibre

Most carpets sold today are blends.

• **Wool** Luxurious, high performance, soft and bulky. Available in many colours. The most expensive carpets are 100 per cent wool and some of the best carpet wool comes from New Zealand. However, all-wool carpets are not as hardwearing as blends. Pure-wool carpets require chemical treatment for moth protection.
• **Linen** Very expensive and not particularly hardwearing. Needs to be used in conjunction with a thick underlay in areas of light traffic.
• **Nylon** The most popular and widely available carpet fibre. Wear-resistant, vivid colours, resilient and stain-resistant. Good-quality nylon is soft; cheap nylon is harsh. More static than natural fibres.
• **Polyester** Creates a soft, thick cut-pile texture. Good colour and easy to maintain. Often used in shag-pile carpet.
• **Polypropylene (olefin)** Durable, stain-resistant and colourfast. A common fibre in Berber carpets. Flattens easily.
• **Acrylic** Similar to wool in appearance and texture, but cheaper. Common in velvet-pile carpets.
• **Viscose** Used in the cheapest carpets. Easily soiled.
• **Blends** One of the most popular carpet types is a wool/nylon blend (4:1), combining the appearance and comfort of wool with nylon's superior wear quality. Other popular blends are acrylic/polypropylene and nylon/polypropylene.

Types of pile

Pile is an important factor in the carpet's texture.

• **Cut pile** Smooth, matt texture that tends to show footmarks.
• **Velvet pile** Very smooth and soft version of cut pile. Hardwearing, but shows footmarks.
• **Loop pile** Pile where the loops are left uncut. Carpets with longer loops are lighter and bulkier.
• **Brussels weave** An expensive, hardwearing loop pile.
• **Cord** Tight low-loop pile. Very hardwearing.
• **Berber** Loop pile made of undyed, variegated or flecked wool.
• **Cut-and-loop pile** A mixture of cut and loop pile to create patterns in relief.
• **Frise-cut pile** Cut pile where the fibres are twisted to tighten the texture. Does not fluff or show footmarks. Hardwearing and good for stairs.
• **Shag pile** Pile up to 50mm long. Hard to keep clean. Suitable for light use only. Do not use on stairs.

Carpet laying

Although a competent amateur might make a decent job of laying foam-backed carpet, laying fabric-backed carpet is definitely a professional's job because the carpet needs to be stretched onto gripper strips.

• Lay carpet over a smooth, level, dry subfloor. Doors may need to be removed and planed to accommodate the pile.
• Foam-backed carpet should be laid over felt paper so that it does not stick to the subfloor.
• Fabric-backed carpet requires underlay. Felt underlays that consist of jute, wool or animal hair, or a combination, are best for woven carpets. Foam or rubber underlays that are noncrumbling are generally used under tufted carpets.

Maintenance

Many carpets are finished with some form of proprietary stain-resistant treatment. Alternatively, this can be applied after the carpet is laid.

• New carpet sheds fluff. Do not vacuum or subject to heavy wear for a few weeks.
• After the carpet has settled down, vacuum regularly (twice a week) to remove dirt.
• Tackle spills immediately, blotting or scraping to remove as much as possible. Then wash gently, working from the outside inwards. Do not scrub or overwet. Treat water-based stains with mild detergent and water; oil-based with dry-cleaning fluid.

Opposite: A flatweave stair carpet provides colour and extra cushioning.
Overleaf:
1. Oatmeal Berber carpet. 2. Carpet woven with leather strips. 3. Wool bouclé. 4. Carpet woven with leather strips. 5. Steel-grey wool carpet. 6. Carpet woven with leather strips. 7. Berber carpet. 8. Taupe carpet with diagonal weave. 9. Patterned wool carpet with relief design.

4

5

6

contemporary

contemporary
introduction

Many contemporary materials derive from the nondomestic contexts of the retail, commercial and industrial sectors. Materials developed for their utility first and foremost have found their way into the home, bringing a clean-lined aesthetic that is much in tune with the principles and precepts of modernism. This creative crossover is not new – it dates back to the Bauhaus, the work of Le Corbusier, Mies van der Rohe, Charles and Ray Eames, and other pioneering designers of the early twentieth century. But it is only in recent decades that the use of such materials has become more mainstream. One of the key factors in broadening the appeal of what might be called 'nondomestic' materials has been the trend for loft-living. Conversions of light industrial warehouses, factories and other redundant commercial properties seemed to call for a more robust approach to surfaces and finishes – materials that would not only evoke a building's utilitarian past, but also acknowledge the dramatic scale of such spaces. In the first wave of loft-living, this response gave us high-tech, a self-consciously direct borrowing of materials, fittings and fixtures from decidedly nondomestic sources.

But it hasn't all been about the shock of the new or the unexpected. The vogue for minimalism stripped interiors back to basics, which necessarily meant a greater degree of attention was paid to the uncluttered sweep of floors and other surfaces. Contemporary approaches to interior design tend to shy away from softer materials, along with clutter, with the result that sound can be amplified to an uncomfortable degree and the overall ambience may be a little hard and chilly. Expanses of concrete can be somewhat dehumanizing, while whole walls infilled with glass may generate a feeling of exposure rather than exhilaration. Tempering more uncompromising materials with those that have warmth, both in visual and practical terms, strikes a good balance.

What many of these materials have in common, along with their modernist edge, is that they are subject to an on-going process of refinement. Concrete that is lightweight, even translucent, and glass that is available in every colour are just some of the improvements of recent years. With decoration entering the digital age, a more playful approach to pattern and design is emerging that marries wit and vitality with the latest in materials technology.

Above: A metal treadplate staircase with mesh balustrading
makes a dramatic feature in a contemporary space.

concrete

Over the past few decades, concrete has been transformed from a material almost universally loathed outside avant-garde architectural circles to one that has found a wide range of applications as a desirable element of the contemporary interior. Exposed concrete walls, floors and built-in features such as counters, sinks and worktops have demonstrated that in the right setting, and with the right finish, concrete can have a robust, monumental beauty.

Concrete's chief role is as a basic construction material and its association with many unlovely aspects of the urban environment – from tower blocks to car parks – has contributed to its conventional image as a dreary, soulless, weather-stained material. Domestically it had only limited applications until relatively recently – as foundations, subfloors, blockwork, lintels and other structural elements, or as utility flooring in areas of the home not intended for public display.

All this changed with the adoption of exposed concrete as a final interior finish by cutting-edge designers. At first, it was the defiant brutality of the material that captured the imagination – concrete's modernist machismo allied with its conspicuous 'poverty' gave extra punch to pared-down minimal interiors. But over the years concrete has acquired ever more sophistication. Finishes that range from a suede-like texture to a smooth polished sheen have brought new subtleties into play, while technological developments have led to forms of concrete that are easier to install on a smaller, domestic scale. Most recently, strange as it may seem, concrete has also become the vehicle for decorative expression.

Opposite: Concrete has edgy contemporary chic.

Characteristics

• As a construction material, concrete's chief advantages are that it is cheap, incredibly strong and capable of being formed into many different shapes.

• Like stone, concrete is dense and massive, which means that it absorbs heat slowly and releases it slowly, an asset in schemes designed to exploit passive solar loss or gain.

• Concrete is fireproof and virtually indestructible if properly made.

• Naturally moisture- and insect-resistant.

• Cold, hard and noisy.

• Stains readily if not sealed or finished in some way; otherwise requires little maintenance.

• Density, appearance and performance are functions of the basic concrete mix. The primary ingredients are sand, water, gravel and Portland cement, all abundant and readily available. However, the production of Portland cement releases carbon dioxide in significant amounts; an eco-friendly alternative is to substitute a proportion of fly ash, waste from coal-powered plants, for the Portland cement.

• New types of concrete include translucent concrete; advanced pre-cast concrete for counters, stairs and other interior features; and lightweight concrete – lighter concrete blocks are more insulating and of necessity use less of the material.

• Concrete can be laid in situ or is available in pre-cast slabs and tiles, in blocks and in thin wall panels.

• Mixing and laying concrete are professional skills. Splashes of wet concrete burn the skin; protective clothing must be worn.

• A range of finishes can be achieved by various means; patterns may be incised into the face of the material and dyes can be added to the mix for colour.

• All concrete that is to be left exposed should be treated to prevent it from 'dusting' or continually breaking down into fine particles.

1

1. Exposed cast-in-situ concrete walls and partitions.
2. An exposed concrete wall on a staircase.

cast in situ

Much of the concrete used in construction is cast in situ (mixed and laid on site). On large schemes, where there is plenty of room to manoeuvre, this is not problematic, but in a domestic setting there can be drawbacks. Work is inevitably messy and requires some plant. Wet concrete needs time to 'cure' and attain maximum hardness, so areas will necessarily be out of bounds.

Mixing concrete is a job for a professional. If there is too little sand or too much water, the concrete will not be dense or strong enough. If there is too much cement, the concrete will be prone to cracking and shrinkage. The more aggregate (sand and gravel) in the mix, the less dense the concrete.

Different types and proportions of aggregate also affect final appearance. Standard concrete is grey; whiter concrete can be achieved by using white cement and white gravel.

Characteristics
• A basic type of concrete with all the common characteristics (see page 101).
• Can be transformed into a structural material (for example, for foundations) by pouring over steel rods, wire or mesh.
• Stains easily.
• Can be coloured by adding pigment to the basic mix.
• Mixing cement with water generates a chemical reaction – wet concrete will burn the skin.
• Sets in hours, but requires up to a month to cure fully.

• Concrete must cure at an even rate, so temperatures must be stable. It will not set if it has been mixed near freezing point.

Applications
• To create foundations or screeded subfloors to provide an even base for subsequent floor coverings, especially heavy materials such as stone and ceramic. Suitable for use over underfloor heating.
• Concrete can be formed into shapes by pouring it into moulds. This 'formwork' (metal or more commonly timber) supports the concrete while it cures and is then removed, leaving a print of its surface behind. 'Shuttered' concrete displays the marks of wooden boarding on its surface.

• As fitted or fixed elements, such as baths, sinks, plinths, tables and worktops.

Finish
• For a smooth surface, rough concrete can be covered with a sand and cement screed.
• Concrete that includes special aggregate can be ground and polished for a look not unlike terrazzo.
• Concrete is porous and will stain if it is not finished in some way. Seal with a self-levelling acrylic or epoxy resin for a glossy, tough and chemical-resistant finish.
• Special concrete floor paints come in a range of colours.
• Industrial toppings designed to make concrete nonslip should be applied by a professional.

2

1

blocks, tiles, panels & slabs

Pre-cast concrete elements, made off site, range from utilitarian products used in construction to more attractive components that are very much designed to be seen. Concrete in this more manageable format cuts short the time on site, as there is no lengthy wait for the material to cure and installation is much less disruptive and messy. However, working with pre-cast concrete elements does require skill and some strength.

New techniques, including photo-etching and CNC (computer numerical control) milling, have the potential to broaden the aesthetic characteristics of concrete immensely by transferring graphics and other images to the surface of tiles and panels. One artist-maker has begun using CNC milling to create floor and wall tiles incised with a three-dimensional design that is derived from rose-patterned lace. Handmade to order, such products bring an industrial material into the realm of artisanship. Bespoke concrete is naturally more expensive than standard off-the-shelf pre-cast elements, but still well within an affordable range.

Decorative concrete tiles are not limited to one-off commissions. A number of companies produce ranges of concrete floor and wall tiles that have great depth of character. Colours are generally earthy or fall within the stone palette of buff, slate-grey, cream and ochre. Textures may be honed smooth or ribbed, and grouting can be treated as part of the overall design of the finished surface.

Characteristics

• Honeycombed concrete 'breeze' blocks have a high insulation rating. They are also easier to manipulate because they are relatively lightweight compared with other pre-cast elements. These are bedded in mortar like bricks.
• Concrete slabs and floor tiles are available in a variety of sizes and thicknesses to suit different applications. Some are textured and coloured to resemble stone. Larger slabs and those used for external paving or terracing are thicker to resist weathering. Thinner floor tiles are laid like other heavy materials by bedding in a mortar mix, the joints pointed after the mortar has set.
• Concrete panels come in a range of thicknesses, the thickest designed for exterior use. Thin tiles can be stuck in place with proprietary adhesive; thicker panels are secured by metal fixings.

Applications

• Concrete 'breeze' blocks are commonly used in masonry construction to form foundation walls, cavity walls, exterior walls and internal partitions. Laid so that the honeycombed surface faces outwards, they can also be

2

used to make semi-transparent screens and garden walls.

• Basic concrete floor tiles make unpretentious flooring in utility areas; bespoke designs are worthy of attention. The subfloor must be strong enough to bear the weight, dry and even.

• Thicker concrete tiles and slabs are commonly used as garden paving.

• Concrete wall tiles and fascia panels can be used to clad walls indoors and out. Again, bespoke or more decorative versions are available.

Finish

• Concrete can stain.

• Special concrete toppings and paints are available.

1. Concrete tiles incised with a floral pattern by Jethro Macey. The pattern is produced by CNC (computer numerical control) milling.
2. Wall made of concrete breeze blocks.

translucent concrete

Concrete is the epitome of a massive, dense material. Its solidity suggests weight and bulk while its rugged appearance has a certain brutal utilitarian aesthetic. Developed by Áron Losonczi, a Hungarian inventor, light-transmitting concrete stands our notion of the material on its head. The translucency of the concrete is supplied by glass or plastic fibres that run parallel through the blocks, admitting light and allowing shadowed shapes to be visible through the material. The diameter of the fibres varies, but because they represent only a tiny percentage of the material, the resulting blocks perform very similarly to standard varieties and can be used structurally as well as decoratively. The material is therefore both hard and strong in compression and semi-see-through.

Characteristics

• Translucent concrete, available in different sizes of block and panel, and as prefabricated elements. Patterns and designs can also be specified.

• Structural performance is similar to standard concrete block.

• Fibres will transmit light effectively up to 20m, which means that walls can be several metres thick with no loss of translucency.

Applications

• External or internal walls or screens. Can be used to bring natural light into windowless spaces.

• Light is intensified if the blocks are sited on east- or west-facing sides because the rays will enter at a lower angle.

• Interior panels are highly effective when backlit.

Opposite: A translucent concrete window screen made of 'Litracon™'.

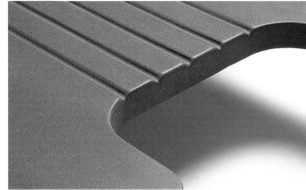

2

3

1

advanced cast concrete

Pre-cast concrete surfaces and finishes combine high-tech practicality with a sleek contemporary aesthetic. Panels, counters, stairs and similar features can be produced to individual specification and installed with a minimum of disruption. As well as standard grey, a range of other colours are also available.

The basic material is a composite of complex cements and natural silica sands. It is produced in sheet form in varying dimensions, profiles and thicknesses. Strong, dense, but with a lightweight core, the material is just as durable as other heavy materials such as stone, but weighs much less. Polished and sealed in the factory, it is ready for installation without the attendant mess, dust and disruption of cast-in-situ concrete.

Characteristics
• Lightweight durable sheets in various thicknesses and sizes.
• The silky smooth surface is cooler than laminate, warmer than stone.
• Easier to install than heavier materials or cast-in-situ concrete.
• Bespoke designs are possible.

Applications
• Kitchen and vanity counters are manufactured with sink and hob cutouts and incised draining grooves. They can also be supplied ready-backed with fibreboard to promote easy installation. The surface is heat- and stain-resistant and antimicrobial.
• Thin concrete sheets are available in large formats to use as wall cladding. Different textures can be stipulated.
• Stair treads and risers can be specified in a number of different shapes and sizes.
• Other uses include tabletops, garden furniture, shelves, hearths and splashbacks.

Finish
• Most types are ready-sealed and stain-resistant.

1. Pre-cast concrete worktop.
2. Inset drainage grooves. Advanced cast concrete is easier to install.
3. Concrete vanity unit.
4. Bespoke concrete counter and supports.
5. Incised floral pattern in advanced cast concrete.

4

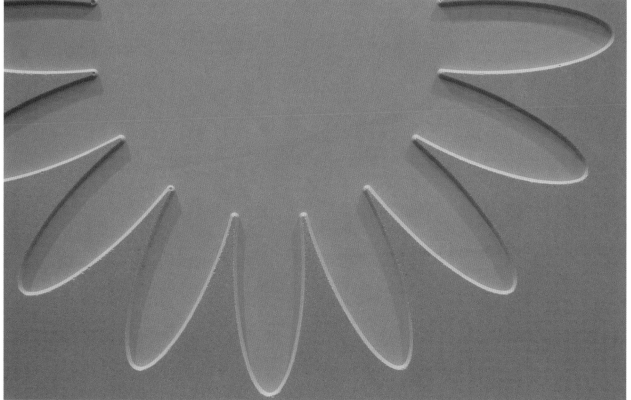

5

1

2

terrazzo

The most upmarket concrete is terrazzo. The basic composition is the same – aggregate mixed with concrete or cement – but the nature of the aggregate, marble or granite chippings, is what gives the surface its beauty, with the natural stone contributing flecks of vivid colour and luminosity. Coloured glass may also be included in the mix.

Cool and chic, and especially welcome in hot climates as flooring, terrazzo's image, nevertheless, has suffered because of its widespread use in commercial and retail settings. Outside Mediterranean areas and other warm regions, you are still more likely to encounter it on a visit to your local supermarket or in other public spaces that see heavy traffic.

Formats

Terrazzo is either laid in situ or comes in the form of slabs and tiles. In both cases, installation is a professional job.

Laid in situ, terrazzo is mixed and then trowelled onto a solid subfloor (concrete or screeded concrete) to form panels separated by brass or zinc dividing strips. It is then ground smooth and surface imperfections levelled with cement paste before being left to cure. After curing it is polished.

Tiles are easier to install. These are generally laid in the same way as other hard tiles, but in groups separated by brass or zinc dividing strips. Some tiles are ground smooth after laying.

Characteristics

• Cold, hard and noisy. The chill of terrazzo is an asset in warmer climates. Objects that drop are more likely to break.
• Standard terrazzo is light-coloured with a mottled patterning that derives from the aggregate of marble, granite and glass employed in its composition. Handmade Mediterranean terrazzo tiles come in a wider range of colours and in geometric designs.
• Patterns and motifs can be created by using tiles of contrasting colour.
• Terrazzo is almost as costly as the best stone. Terrazzo laid in situ is more expensive than tiles.
• Very durable.
• Reasonably nonslip unless polished or wet.

Applications

• The principal application of terrazzo is for flooring, especially in kitchens, bathrooms, halls and other places where a very durable surface is required.

Finish

• Seal with water-based dressing to protect against stains.
• Avoid polishes that contain wax and which might make the floor excessively slippery.
• Wash with warm water and cleanser. Soap leaves a slippery film.

1. Terrazzo floor showing oval motifs.
2. Terrazzo is very hardwearing.
3.–6. Terrazzo comes in a range of colours and patterning, depending on the aggregate used in its composition.

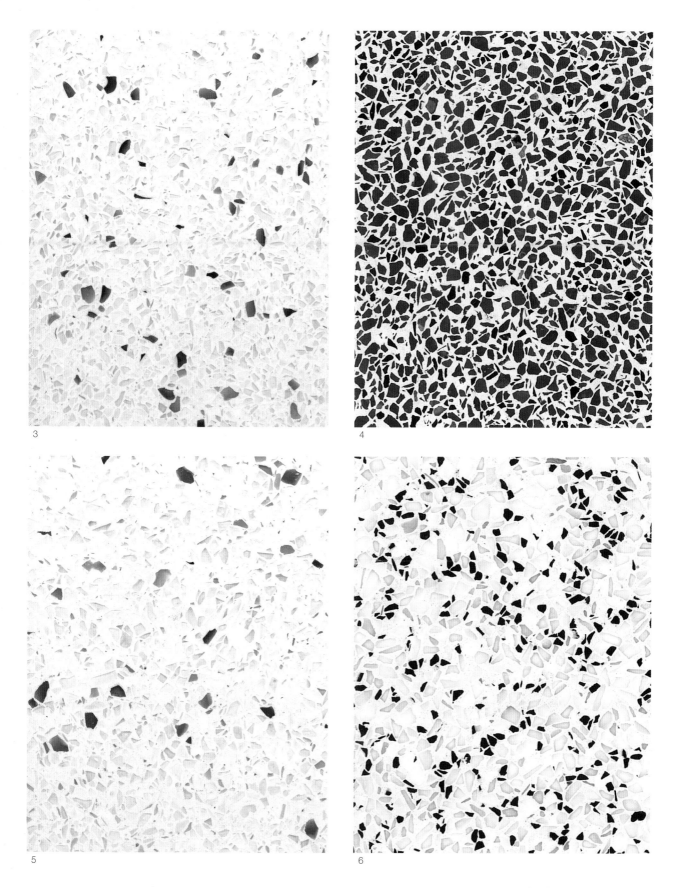

3

4

5

6

metal

While metal has been present in our homes for many centuries, this has generally been on the smallest of scales – as nails, screws, bolts, catches, handles and other fixings, or in the form of details, from fire screens to balustrading. What is relatively new is the presence of metal both as an expressed structural element and, newer still, its use as a cladding to cover substantial surface areas. In these latter roles metal has a sharp, modern edge, particularly in partnership with glass.

As an interior surface, metal brings an industrial aesthetic into the home with overtones of aeronautical design. Its reflective surface suggests hygiene and efficiency, as exemplified by the professional-style stainless-steel kitchen. Even in relatively limited applications – to form an upper-level walkway or a spiral staircase, for instance – the material adds a certain crispness of definition.

Types of metal
All metals, however much processing subsequently goes into their production, come from ores mined from the earth. There are two basic types: noble metals and base metals. Noble metals include gold, silver, copper and mercury and are found in a pure state. Base metals, such as iron, lead and aluminium, tend to react when exposed to the air.

Characteristics
• All types of metal are good conductors of heat and electricity. They warm up quickly and lose heat quickly.
• Metal has great strength.
• Amplifies sound if used extensively as a cladding.
• Durable and pest-resistant.
• As a group, metals have a tendency to rust or corrode. Protecting metal with an applied finish is one solution, another is to use metal in stable alloys (such as stainless steel).
• Metal is relatively expensive as a structural material. However, because of its strength it can be formed into fairly minimal framing, so less of the material is required.

Eco factors
• Metal is high in embodied energy, more than 300 times that of timber.
• Extraction and mining of metal can spoil landscapes and habitats.
• Metal processing is a key polluter.
• Because the material is so strong, it can be used minimally, and metal frames and cladding are used in many green buildings. If frames are bolted rather than welded together, this facilitates reuse.
• Metal is easy to recycle. There are good recycling rates for many types of metal because the material is so expensive. Steel that is 90 per cent recycled is available in many different products, from structural beams to nails.

Opposite: Lightweight spiral metal staircase with perforated treads.

1

2

3

iron

As a metal that has been worked for millennia, iron has given its name to one of the three principal ages of early human technological development, the Iron Age, which succeeded the Bronze Age as the superior qualities of iron for fashioning tools and weapons were demonstrated. For centuries most metal artefacts were made of iron and the generic term 'ironmongery' continues to be used for a variety of utilitarian metal products whether they are made of iron or not. There are abundant iron deposits around the world, the largest in North and South America.

Types of iron

• The basic form of all types of iron is pig iron. It is extracted from the ore in a blast furnace at a temperature of 1,300°C. Steel is composed of 98–99 per cent pig iron.

• Cast iron is strong in compression, but brittle and rigid. It is shaped when molten by pouring it into moulds. It is more resistant to corrosion than wrought iron. Most iron artefacts and structural members post-industrialization are made of cast iron.

• Wrought iron is strong in tension, and can be pulled, twisted and worked into shapes. To make wrought iron, iron oxide is added to molten pig iron to purify it and make it less liquid. In a semi-molten state, wrought iron can be hammered and stretched. Before industrialization, most ironmongery was made of wrought iron at the blacksmith's forge. Today wrought iron is chiefly limited to decorative applications.

• Corrugated iron was invented and patented in Britain in the 1820s. The corrugations give the iron sheeting strength and this form of the material rapidly found a use in temporary structures, agricultural buildings and other types of utility cladding all around the world. Today the term is often used to refer to corrugated sheeting made of other metals such as steel.

Characteristics

• High melting point.

• Exceptionally hard.

4

- Very heavy.
- Abundant and relatively cheap.
- Easy to recycle.
- Corrodes relatively easily if not protected by a finish.

Applications

Many of iron's applications in the interior are in the form of period or reproduction features and fittings.

- Handles, catches, latches, doorknockers and other door and cabinetry furniture.
- Fire surrounds, fire irons, fireguards, pokers.
- Glazing bars in original period windows and conservatories.
- Columns and beams (cast iron) in reclaimed warehouses and other buildings.
- Balustrading and railings.
- Spiral staircases (cast iron).

Finish

- Like all base metals, iron is prone to rusting, a process that is naturally accelerated when it is used out of doors. A protective coat of metal paint or lacquer is the standard finish. Galvanizing or zinc plating increases corrugated iron's resistance to rust, but painting gives full protection.

1. Corrugated-iron roofing in a house in Palm Springs.
2. Cast-iron pillar, a typical feature of old warehouses and commercial buildings.
3. Corrugated-iron ceiling.
4. Feature wall made of strips of iron in a contemporary Italian house.

1

2

steel

Steel is truly the workhorse material of the modern world. It has innumerable applications, from saucepans to suspension bridges. In architectural terms, the development of steel as a structural material was one of the factors that led to the emergence of the skyscraper as a building form. But as well as enabling us to build higher and higher, steel frameworks have allowed buildings to be lighter and airier. Minimal structural frames mean that walls can be infills of glass and layouts can be open and free of divisions.

Steel is produced by refining pig iron to remove a proportion of its carbon content as well as other impurities. This is achieved either by oxidation or by the electro-steel process, in which scrap iron and steel are melted in an electric furnace and subjected to further refinement. Once the molten steel cools into ingots, it can then be levelled, cut, profiled and shaped in countless ways.

Types of steel
The most basic form of steel, carbon steel, is commonly used in the construction industry. But there are many other types, alloys in which the presence of other metals enhance certain aspects of performance.

• Stainless steel is one of the most expensive types of steel. Unlike carbon steel, which is prone to corrosion, stainless steel, an alloy containing chromium and nickel, will not rust and is easy to maintain.

• Adding manganese to steel makes it more impact-resistant.

• Adding tungsten to steel makes it able to withstand high temperatures.

• Galvanized steel is coated with a layer of zinc, which makes it weatherproof.

• Weathering steel (trademark Cor-ten®) has a coating of iron, phosphorus, carbon and copper, which breaks down into a protective rust layer over the surface of the material.

• Corrugated-steel sheet is usually covered with aluminium, zinc or both.

Characteristics
• Steel is much stronger than iron, but in its nonalloy form (carbon steel) it is very susceptible to corrosion.

• Steel is pliable, which considerably broadens its range of applications.

• Recycling is well established because of steel's relatively high value.

• Available in hundreds of different types of alloys, as well as with many different coatings and finishes.

• Relief textures, such as corrugating, gridding and ridging, increase the structural strength of steel sheet.

• Special coatings can be applied to steel to increase fire-resistance.

Applications
• As structural frameworks. Steel framing has the potential

3

4

5

to create light and airy spaces with optimum-sized openings – or fully glazed walls. Steel beams (RSJs or rolled steel joists) are commonly used in a load-bearing capacity to compensate for areas of load-bearing masonry walls that have been removed.

• Steel-framed windows and doors. Metal-framed windows, however, are not environmentally friendly, as they tend to form cold bridges that can compromise insulation and lead to condensation and mould.

• To form upper mezzanine levels, stairs and walkways. A number of firms specialize in custom-made steel stairs.

• As flooring. Galvanized steel tiles or sheet can be applied over a level subfloor, either by adhesive or by screwing into position. Steel tiles backed with rigid board are easy to install and come in a range of different finishes.

• As cladding. Stainless-steel panels make excellent cladding for kitchen cabinets and baths, as well as worksurfaces and splashbacks. These thin sheets are widely available in standard sizes and formats and can be stuck in place. Alternatively, you can also use steel tiles (see above).

• As fixtures and fittings. These include sinks, washbasins, lavatories, taps, handles and a host of other interior features, from furniture to storage boxes.

Finish

• Steel is available in a wide range of coatings to resist corrosion. Under normal conditions and in areas not exposed to moisture, steel will not rust indoors.

• Stainless-steel surfaces tend to show spotting and grease streaks. Use a manufacturer's recommended cleaning product to restore a gleaming finish.

1. A steel-mesh window cover screens the light and provides security.
2. Heavy steel door.
3. Sleek steel-clad kitchen island.
4. Steel-frame extension.
5. Polished steel handrail and balustrade.

1

2   1. Aluminium kitchen units. 2. Perforated-aluminium wall cupboards.

aluminium, zinc & copper

Aluminium Worldwide, the use of aluminium exceeds that of any other metal except iron, and accordingly it plays a big part in the global economy. Its role in aeronautical engineering is well known – as a lightweight metal, aluminium is widely used in the manufacture of aircraft components. But it also plays a role in construction and as an interior finish.

Characteristics
• Dull silvery appearance that is the result of oxidation.
• Very lightweight – up to three times lighter than steel.
• Resistant to corrosion. Anodized aluminium thickens the corrosion-resistant film that forms with oxidation.
• Soft and malleable.

Aluminium is the second most malleable metal after gold.
• Good conductor of heat and electricity.
• Nonmagnetic.
• Available in relief-patterned sheets known as treadplate.
• Anodized aluminium has a porous surface that can be dyed a range of colours.
• Heat-tempered aluminium is as strong, hard and resilient as steel.
• Aluminium is most commonly available as alloys.

Applications
• As flooring. Treadplate aluminium sheet and tiles are much lighter than steel. They can be fixed with adhesive or by screwing into place. Aluminium flooring can be noisy

and has a tendency to rattle.
• Window and doorframes.
• As blinds and spatial dividers.
• Siding.
• As lightweight furniture and other small-scale applications.

Finish
• Aluminium is highly resistant to corrosion and requires no further treatment except basic maintenance.

Zinc A bluish-white metal, zinc is naturally resistant to corrosion. More than half of the zinc produced is used to galvanize steel and protect it from rusting. Contrary to popular belief, the characteristic material used to cover Parisian bar counters is not zinc, even though such bars are

commonly known as 'zinc bars'. Instead, the material is an alloy of tin and lead.

Characteristics
• Naturally resistant to corrosion.
• Soft and easily scratched.
• Pliable.
• Durable.
• Widely used in alloys. Zinc alloyed with copper makes brass.

Applications
• The most common application of zinc is to galvanize or plate other metals, usually steel.
• In construction, zinc is used to make roofing, flashing, gutters and downpipes.
• Zinc panels can be used to clad doors or worksurfaces.

3   3. Traditional copper-clad soaking tub. 4. Copper-clad shower enclosure. 5. Zinc cladding used on a roof extension.

4

Finish

Zinc requires no subsequent finishing. With time and use, surfaces will acquire a patina of scratch marks.

Copper The only brown metal, copper has warm, rich tones and a reflective surface that give it an attractive homely quality. Its use in the interior remains rather limited and it requires more maintenance than other metals.

Characteristics

• Fairly resistant to corrosion.
• Good conductor of electricity.
• Available in a variety of finishes – smooth, hammered or relief-patinated.
• Copper alloyed with tin makes bronze.

Applications

• As a roofing material.
• As decorative fireplace hoods and other fireplace features.
• Copper has traditionally been used to make sinks and baths.
• Copper panels can be applied to kitchen units and other surfaces. As is the case with steel, copper tiles are available backed with a rigid board that makes them easy to install.

Finish

• Copper tarnishes easily, discolouring to a greenish tone. Regular cleaning with a proprietary product is necessary to preserve the warm colour and shiny finish.

5

1

metal mesh & metal fabrics

Perforated or woven metal lightens the basic material and gives it a greater degree of transparency. The lightest metal mesh or metal fabric has a gauzy quality similar to fine-weight textiles and can be used in similar applications. Metal mesh designed for architectural uses has a crisp, refined aesthetic.

Characteristics

• Specification varies enormously according to the type of metal used and the way it is worked. At one end of the scale, metal mesh can be rigid, durable, dense and heavy; at the other, it can be flexible, delicate, light and open. Mesh can also be designed so that it is flexible in one direction only, or in two.

• Metals used include stainless steel, copper, brass and bronze.
• Mesh has high tensile strength.
• Woven metal cloth is made by crossing fine metal wires at right angles, crimping them in the process to make firm connections. Very fine mesh can be achieved this way. Specialty fabrics are available in a range of weights and designs.
• Metal mesh has a relative degree of transparency.

Applications

• Stairs and walkways. More rigid forms of metal mesh and perforated panels make excellent stair treads, upper walkways and balustrading. The lightness is an asset where a solid metal might impose too great a load;

the transparency preserves views across interior spaces, a particular advantage when dividing a space vertically by adding a mezzanine level, for example.

• As screening and dividers. A variety of different types of metal mesh can be used to screen areas minimally, for security purposes or as external panels. There are many ways of installing mesh, depending on its degree of flexibility. It can be framed in metal frameworks, supported by threaded rods or hung from loops.

• Woven metal fabric shares many of the same applications as textiles. The shimmering quality of the material adds luminosity to window

treatments. One company makes cushion covers from metal cloth. Their heat-retaining properties provide an extra element of comfort.

Finish

• A number of different coatings can be applied, including paint.
• Mesh may also be anodized to resist corrosion.

1. Gauzy metal fabric.
2. A wall hung with metal chain.

2

glass

Glass has been subject to a continuous process of refinement and the modern material bears little resemblance, either in appearance or technical specification, to early forms, which were restricted in size and clouded with impurities. One of the big technological breakthroughs came with developments in plate glass in the early twentieth century, which enabled the material to be manufactured economically on a much bigger scale. Coinciding with improvements to steel, which meant that it could be used to form relatively minimal structural frameworks, this resulted in buildings whose glass walls literally dissolved the boundaries between inside and out.

A similar revolution in glass technology has taken place in recent years and there are many different types of glass on the market today to suit a wide range of applications. Smart (reactive) glass and eco glass are covered in later sections (see pages 168–73 and 216–21); included here are a number of types of glass that have particular relevance in design and decorative contexts.

Glass is a key element in contemporary design. Increasingly, preferences are for open interior spaces and plenty of natural light; expanses of glass infilling generous openings is one of the principal ways of delivering this type of spatial quality. But glass has other applications, too; the availability of strengthened glass, in particular, has seen glass used in innovative ways – as flooring or transparent baths and sinks, for example.

Most of the glass produced today is 'float glass'. During manufacture, the molten glass is poured onto a bath of molten tin where it levels out, cools and hardens. After subsequent hardening in an annealing lehr, the resulting glass is perfectly flat, uniform in thickness and has polished surfaces. Rolled glass, another basic type, is used to make wired and patterned glass. During this process, semi-molten glass is pressed between rollers.

Characteristics

• With the exception of coloured or overtly decorative glass, many types of glass do not appear superficially very different from one another. Performance, however, can vary widely, so it is always important to take advice when considering glass for a specific application.

• Available in a range of sizes and thicknesses. Larger sheets are of necessity thicker. Maximum size is determined by the limitations of shipping and handling.

• Large expanses of glass are heavy and framing or edge detailing are key considerations. Installation is a professional job.

• With the exception of self-cleaning glass, most types of glass require significant degrees of maintenance to remain in a pristine, sparkling condition.

• With the exception of low-E (low-emissivity) glass (see pages 217–18), expanses of glazing tend to overheat interiors during warm weather and drain heat at night or during the cooler months.

• Glass is readily recycled with no loss of quality.

Opposite: Coloured laminated safety glass drenches a children's play area with bright vibrant shades.

1

2

strengthened glass

Many of the recent innovations in glass technology have addressed its fragility and brittleness. Standard glass shatters very easily, particularly on impact, creating dangerously sharp shards that can wound very severely. It is also, for that reason, far from secure (though the noise of breakage can deter intruders, particularly at the front of properties where they are more likely to be overheard, and large expanses of glass may also be daunting because of the safety risk). As glass has been used in greater quantities, for both external openings and internal divisions, and in larger sizes, its strength has become an ever more important consideration.

Glass can be strengthened only up to a point. After that, it has to be a question of ensuring that if and when it does break, it fractures into harmless pebbles.

Types of strengthened glass
• Wired glass One of the most basic and cheapest forms of strengthened glass is wired glass. Rather like the wire mesh that forms the reinforcing element in structural concrete, fine steel mesh inserted between two layers of glass increases its strength. It also serves the purpose of holding fragments in place after the glass is shattered. Wired glass is not fully secure, but it is tough enough to deter opportunistic break-ins.

• Toughened glass
Toughened or tempered glass, as it is also known, is produced by heating glass to 650°C then rapidly chilling it, with the result that the outer layers of glass solidify before the core. As the core cools, the outer layers are compressed. Toughened glass is five times stronger than standard glass and breaks into small harmless pieces. It cannot be worked after toughening, so must be made to size.
• Laminated glass More expensive than toughened glass, laminated glass consists of a layer of plastic sandwiched between the glass layers. After impact, the plastic layer holds the fragments in place. Laminated glass was first

developed for car windows and has the best safety specification.
• Toughened and laminated glass Various combinations of different types of glass, in different thicknesses and numbers of layers, are also available for optimum strength. Bulletproof glass, for example, consists of multiple layers of toughened and laminated glass.
• Honeycombed glass Glass incorporating honeycombed aluminium is light, rigid and strong enough to be used structurally and in flooring applications. It comes in clear, sandblasted and coloured versions.

3

Applications

• Use strengthened glass in any area that is vulnerable to impact or break-ins: glazed panels in external doors, ground-floor windows, internal glazed partitions, French windows and the like. One of the risks associated with glass is that it is so transparent that it is less immediately visible as a barrier.

• Flooring, upper walkways and stairs. A general specification for flooring glass is a top layer 19mm thick laminated to a 10m-thick base; honeycombed glass is an alternative. Sandblasted spots or friction bars cut down on slipperiness. Most flooring glass is available in metre-square panels so that it can be handled more easily. The supporting framework generally includes

a neoprene rubber cushioning.

• Glass beams can be used to support glazed roofs for a fully transparent look.

• Strengthened glass is used to make glass baths and sinks. Water and glass is a beguiling combination and glass minimizes the scale of what can be bulky fixtures.

• Shower enclosures, screening for built-in storage and balustrading.

• Worktops, tabletops, splashbacks and vanity tops. Edges must be bevelled or rounded to prevent accidents.

1. Glass spiral staircase.
2. Detail of glass stair treads.
3. Cantilevered transparent box made of strengthened glass.
4. External walkway made of textured strengthened glass.

4

1

decorative glass

The whole point about glass is its transparency, its ability to admit natural light and provide views from inside to outside or create interior vistas. In some circumstances, however, full transparency is not welcome, either for security reasons or to provide a greater degree of privacy. In other cases, glass plays a more purely decorative role, contributing colour, pattern and texture in various ways.

Types of decorative glass

• **Coloured glass** Glass can be coloured in a variety of ways. At the most basic, it can be hand-painted or enamelled with special glass paint – the colour is very obviously on the surface, though the effects can be quite subtle. Most coloured glass available commercially is made by adding metal oxides to the molten material, so that the glass is tinted or 'stained' through with colour. Colours can be remarkably jewel-like and intense, but the range of shades available is generally not particularly large. Strengthened glass used in cladding or roofing can be enamelled, with the colour added in the form of mineral pigments sprayed to the back of the glass, or the colour may reside in the resin that binds individual glass layers together. In either case, colour choice is very wide. An alternative is coloured laminated safety glass (see page 128) where the colour is delivered via a plastic interlayer. Colouring glass lowers the level of light that shines through and increases the ability of the glass to absorb heat, hence interiors are cooler as well as darker.

• **Opaque glass** Opaque or translucent glass has a matt appearance and reduced transparency, so views are obscured. Light is not blocked, but gently diffused. To achieve opacity or translucency, the surface of the glass is either acid-etched or sandblasted. For greater decorative effect, it is possible to commission designs, ranging from simple geometric shapes – squares, dots and so on – to more elaborate patterns. These are masked onto the glass before etching.

• **Patterned glass** Screen-printing extends the decorative range. Repeating patterns, graphics or pictorial motifs can be transferred to glass of varying sizes. A wide range of inks specifically intended for use with glass are available, in transparent and opaque colours. Screen-printing can also be used to apply temporary coatings as a mask during sandblasting or etching.

• **Textured glass** Obscured or textured glass features relief patterns or surface texture that reduces transparency and distorts views. This type of glass is produced either by casting or by impressing the design on the semi-molten surface of the glass with a roller.

2

3

4

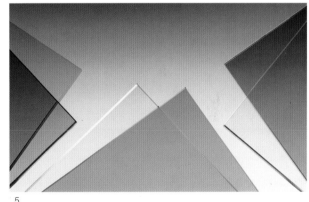

5

Applications

• As a decorative element in its own right. Slivers of coloured or textured glass can be very effective in door panels, as transoms or as upper panels in glazed rooms. Where the light shines through, it creates enchanting coloured or dappled shadows.

• To give greater privacy without blocking too much light. Bathroom windows, glazed bathroom doors and front doors with glazing panels are common sites for obscured decorative glass.

• To make glass more visible. Translucent, coloured or textured glass screens and doors are safer than fully transparent ones because they are easier to notice.

• Cladding, dividers, cupboard doors and shower enclosures.

• Counters, worktops, vanity tops and splashbacks.

1. Coloured laminated glass doors on either side of a contemporary chimneybreast are safer than fully transparent ones.
2. Decorative printed-glass splashback.
3. Patterned glass used as a screen.
4. Backlit patterned glass enclosing a bathtub.
5. Samples of coloured glass.

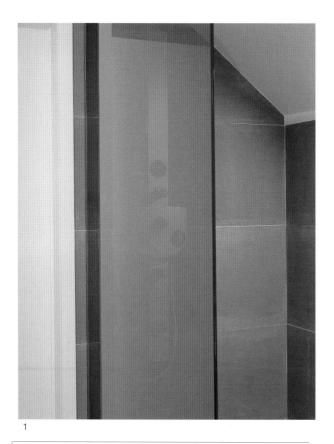

1

2

coloured laminated safety glass

From the luminous stained glass of medieval cathedrals to more recent Victorian, Edwardian and Art Deco embellishments in windows and doors, coloured glass has been around for many centuries, usually in the form of through-coloured glass or glass that is tinted or stained during its manufacture. What is different about coloured laminated safety glass is that the colour is delivered via a film or polyvinylbutyral (PVB) interlayer sandwiched between two sheets of glass. This provides both an incredibly wide choice of colour and a high degree of performance, making the glass suitable for an extensive range of architectural applications.

The glass is available in more than a thousand different transparent and translucent colours. A colour-matching system also allows you to find out the closest shade to any Pantone or other international reference code. Colours are based on pigments rather than dyes, which makes them very stable.

Characteristics
• Huge range of colours, from subtle to brilliant, transparent to translucent.
• Provides a high degree of security and safety as glass fragments adhere to the interlayer in the event of breakage.
• Resistant to exposure and weathering.

3

• Provides acoustic insulation and UV protection.
• Available in different widths and specifications, including double glazing.

Applications
• External or internal glazing: windows, door panels, screens, room dividers, balustrading and balconies.

1. Coloured laminated safety glass is available in a vast range of colours.
2. Bright green glazing on a balcony.
3. Colours are based on pigments, which makes them stable.

1

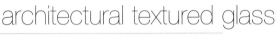

2

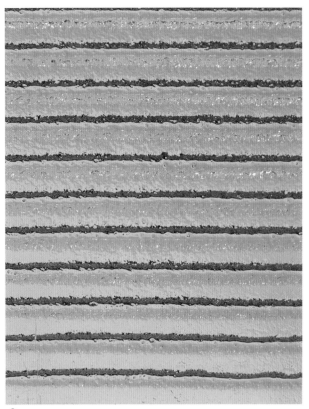

3

architectural textured glass

Textured or 'obscured' glass has typically been used in areas of the home where privacy is required – in glazed front door panels, for example, or bathroom windows. Off-the-shelf designs, however, tend not to be very appealing and the glazing is standard rather than high-performance. Today, however, new types of specialist architectural glass are available that marry textural variety with high specification. Textural patterns can be formed or blasted and unique patterns can be created to individual specification. The effect is particularly striking when backlit. Because textured glass is relatively nonslip it can be used in flooring applications, for walkways and stairs.

Characteristics

• Wide range of textural designs, including special commissions.
• Glazing is toughened so that it is impact-resistant and secure.
• Curved or bent panels can also be produced (however, these cannot be toughened).

Applications

• Exterior and interior glazing: frameless doors, counters, tabletops, cladding, feature walls, shower screens, vanity tops, walkways, balustrading and stairs.

1.–4. Textured glass is available in a range of patterns and designs and to high specification.

4

1

profiled glass systems

One of the drawbacks of using glass extensively as a cladding element, screen or room divider is the difficulty of installation. Large sheets of glass are heavy, prone to damage and require special support and framing. One way of avoiding such problems is to opt for a profiled glass system in which the glazing is composed of many individual glass channels or panels. While the channels are secured around the periphery with an aluminium frame lined in plastic, each directly abuts the other, locking into place via flanges, making installation quick and easy. Commonly used in large-scale commercial and retail projects, such systems can also be applied domestically to create glazed external or internal walls.

Illuminated systems

One striking variant on the theme adds light to the picture. Electroluminescent lamps are enclosed within some or all of the channels to create a glowing backdrop. The light source provides secondary illumination, requires no maintenance and has a long lifespan, dimming gradually over time. Used with colour filters, almost any colour can be achieved. With sandblasted glass, the effect is an even wash of light across the surface. With clear glass, the structure of the wall is emphasized.

Characteristics

• Self-supporting U-shaped glass channels within an aluminium frame.

2

• Can be arranged with the channels running vertically or horizontally. Curves are achieved very easily by faceting the channels into a curved frame.
• Available in different lengths, widths and thickness, and in double and single glazing.
• Wide range of colour and textural options.
• Bespoke solutions available.

Applications

• Extensive areas of glazing – cladding, partitions, dividers and enclosures.
• Curved glass screens and façades.

1. Profiled glass screen.
2. Detail of the glass channels.
3. Profiled glass used to screen a stairway.

1

glass blocks

Glass blocks have been around for some time. One early example of their use is in Pierre Chareau's Maison de Verre (1931) whose façade features a double-height wall entirely constructed of glass blocks. Combining transparency with strength, glass blocks can be used in many different contexts, internally and externally, where you don't want to block light, but a more substantial and secure material is required. In recent years, glass blocks have become something of a cliché in contemporary interiors. Small inserts or panels are not as successful as more wholehearted applications.

Installation is generally a professional job. However, there are new dry-fix walling systems that are simpler to carry out. Continuous plastic profiles are fixed to the floor and wall, and blocks are stuck in place with adhesive. Blocks are not stuck to each other; instead, each block is separated from the next by short lengths of profiled plastic inserted like spacers between them. After the adhesive has settled, the joints between the blocks are filled with flexible filler.

Characteristics

• Strong, durable and secure. Good sound- and heat-insulating qualities.
• Very secure vandalproof blocks are available, as well as fire-resistant types.
• Range of colours and finishes, from clear to rippled, frosted and patterned. A new whiter white block is also available that lacks the characteristic greenish tinge of standard clear glass.
• Generally square in format, but corner blocks are also available.
• Readily formed into curved partitions and enclosures. Quicker to construct than standard masonry.
• Substantial weight. You need to check that the subfloor is strong enough. The base should be perfectly dry and even.

Applications

• As an infill in external openings, especially where additional strength and security are required. Textured blocks also provide a greater degree of privacy as views are obscured.
• As internal walls and partitions. Can run floor to ceiling or half-height or half-width. Curves are easy to achieve.
• As a screen for a bathing area or shower enclosure.
• As pavement or floor lights bringing light down into basement areas.

1. Glass blocks lend themselves to forming curved partitions.
2. A wholehearted use of glass blocks is more successful than small inset panels.

1

mirror

The very earliest mirrors were simply polished sheets of metal. Mirror glass – blown glass backed with silver – remained small in scale until the late seventeenth century when the first large sheets of glass were cast. Today mirror is chiefly made by back-silvering, or coating the back surface of glass with aluminium. To protect the mirror from corrosion, it is then back-painted. Modern backings are much better than those used in earlier mirrors, which have a tendency to wear away and degrade the reflection.

In purely practical terms, mirrors provide us with the information we need for personal hygiene and grooming. It's not simply vanity – it's difficult to apply make-up or shave without seeing what you are doing. But mirror serves other purposes, too. The reflective glitter of mirror has the effect of enhancing the quality of natural light. Positioned carefully, mirror can also set up views and vistas that make spaces seem bigger than they really are.

Characteristics

• Mirror is available in many different formats and styles. Plain sheet mirror can be cut to size or bought off the shelf in standard dimensions. Mirror is also available in a range of shapes, with circular being the most popular.
• Traditional mirrors, whose styles are largely expressed through framing, include freestanding cheval mirrors that tilt, overmantel mirrors incorporating display niches, glittering Venetian mirrors and retro-style Art Deco designs. Angled or three-way mirrors provide a wider view. Original antique mirrors in good condition are extremely expensive; many traditional styles are produced in reproductions of varying quality and authenticity.
• The larger the mirror, the heavier it is. Like standard glass, mirror shatters easily. As an alternative to glass mirror, safety mirror made of acrylic is available for use in large-scale applications. Devised for gyms, dance studios and riding schools, acrylic mirror is lighter, stronger, shatter-resistant and easier to install but of similar reflective quality.
• Mirrors mist up in steamy surroundings. Heated mirrors for bathroom use stay free from condensation.
• Many bathroom cabinets incorporate mirrored fronts; some feature integral lighting to prevent reflections from the surface of the glass and to light the face evenly.
• Mirror is available adhesive-backed in small formats as tiles and mirror mosaic.
• Mirrored furniture was particularly in vogue in the 1920s and 1930s. Original examples can be sourced from antiques shops but command a premium price. Contemporary mirrored furniture is also produced.

2

3

Applications

• As decorative features and focal points, mirrors can be hung and positioned like pictures.

• Plain frameless sheet mirror can be used as a cladding – in alcoves, as splashbacks or to line an entire wall. On a small scale, mirror can be stuck in place with silicone sealant or a recommended mirror adhesive. Larger sheets should be pre-drilled and screwed securely into place. Never stick mirror to the ceiling unless you are certain that it can bear the weight. Most ceilings are simply applied finishes to the underside of the floor structure.

• Mirror tile and mirror mosaic share similar applications to other tiles, but they must never be used on the floor. They are not impact-resistant and they are also far too slippery.

Finish

• Mirror needs no subsequent finishing but, like glass, is demanding in terms of maintenance.

• Unheated mirrors steam up and the surface will show every smudge and finger mark. Clean with a window-cleaning product and a dry cloth.

1. Mirror is a tried-and-tested way of enhancing space.
2. Chic contemporary use of mirror panels.
3. Mirrored wall-hung vanity unit.
4. Sheet mirror in a bathroom.

4

composites

What, for want of a better word, might be called synthetic materials, composites demonstrate our continuing attempts to improve upon nature. Many of these have a short history and none dates back any further than the early decades of the twentieth century. Some are wholly artificial; others combine artificial materials, such as plastic in some form or another, with natural ingredients to gain optimum performance and visual appeal.

Ever since the great explosion in plastics technology after the Second World War, we have had a somewhat ambivalent relationship with synthetic materials, but none more so than today. Plastic is now so ubiquitous in our homes – from light switches to lunch boxes, lavatory seats to damp-proof membranes – that it is hard to imagine how the world survived without it. At the same time, we are learning to count the environmental cost. While plastic can be readily recycled (see pages 222–7), its production is heavily dependent on oil and is far from eco-friendly. Added to which is the fact that the plastic that is not recycled, which remains the overwhelming majority of it, ends up on landfill and is largely not biodegradable.

General features

It is difficult to summarize the characteristics of this group of materials because their performance and specification vary so widely.

• One of the few generalizations that it is fair to make is that synthetics are by and large cheaper than natural or more massive materials.

• Practicality – ease of installation, ease of maintenance, adaptability – tends to score highly, though not necessarily at the expense of good looks.

• Many of these materials were developed for specific applications – as a form of technical problem-solving – but, in the same way that Teflon® originated as a coating in space technology and is now more familiar as the base of nonstick pans, they have often left their original uses long behind them.

• While many synthetics are highly wear-resistant, they lack the ability of natural materials to improve with age and use, and any damage is simply an eyesore.

• What is undoubtedly true is that the advent of synthetic materials has made the world an infinitely more colourful place. Before plastic, bright colour was chiefly the preserve of the well-to-do; now it is everywhere. While many composites are patterned and coloured specifically to ape natural materials, a bright and cheerful aesthetic is generally more successful.

Opposite: Bamboo rings set in sheet-resin panels.

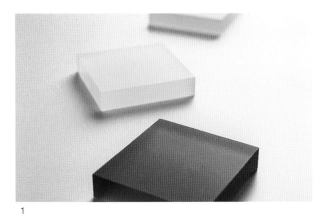

1

2

3

acrylic

Invented in the first wave of plastics technology after the First World War, acrylic is a type of plastic known as a thermoplastic. Thermoplastics, which also include polystyrene, polythene, PVC and nylon, become soft when heated and stiff when cooled. Their flexibility means that they can be formed into complex shapes.

Acrylic, either cast into forms, as sheets and panels, or in the form of resin, crops up in an incredibly diverse range of products, from watch faces to car brake lights, from aquaria to baths. Mixed with pigments and fillers, it can be used to simulate dense natural materials, such as granite, sandstone, limestone, marble and concrete, and formed into bathroom fixtures. Under the trademark Perspex®, it is widely used as a substitute for glass.

Characteristics
• Strong and durable. Acrylic delivers more strength in thin sections than other materials such as ceramic.
• Lightweight, which is an asset both in panels and in solid forms, such as bathroom fixtures.
• Available in a wide range of nonfading colours.
• Warm to the touch.
• Can be opaque, translucent or transparent.
• Transparent acrylic sheet is lighter and shatter-resistant but more expensive than glass. It is also flammable and scratches easily, which compromises optical clarity.

• Cast Perspex sheet is a premium-grade product that offers near optical clarity in its clear form. It also comes in a range of vibrant colours as well as fluorescent and pearlescent shades, and in different surface finishes including glass, silk, dotted and frosted. It can be supplied in stock sizes or cut to any dimension or shape.
• Low maintenance.

Applications
• Bathtubs, sinks, shower trays and other bathroom fittings.
• Acrylic sheet makes a good substitute for glazing, especially in any context where there is a risk that glass might shatter. As it is much lighter than glass, large sheets are easier to install.

Finish
• Acrylic requires little maintenance. Guard against scratches and do not use abrasive scouring powders or cleansers.

1.–2. Samples of acrylic.
3. Bed raised on Perspex legs.
4. Contoured acrylic workstation.

4

1

Corian® & composite stone

Like Perspex®, Corian® is a trademarked product. In the many decades it has been on the market, its name has almost become the generic term for a solid composite material. Comprising a blend of acrylic with natural minerals, it is made into sheets or pre-formed shapes with a widespread application in both the home and public environments.

Totally solid, through-coloured and with no visible seams, Corian is particularly suited to uses in kitchens and bathrooms where a high degree of performance and hygiene is required. Because it is through-coloured, colours and patterns don't wear away or delaminate, as can be the case with other composite sheets.

Characteristics

• Corian comes in 110 different shades, including earth tones, neutrals, bright saturated colours, pure white and black. The colour range is constantly expanding, which makes it easy to match decorative schemes.

• Corian can be carved, routed and drilled like wood. It can also be moulded, thermoformed or inlayed.

• All colours are available in sheets of standard dimensions. Other dimensions are available by special request. Corian is generally used in fairly substantial thickness, but a new 6mm format is now being produced.

• Nontoxic, hypoallergenic and antibacterial, it will not offgas at normal temperatures.

• Nonporous, hardwearing,

2

stain- and moisture-resistant.

• Heat- and impact- resistant.

• A range of pre-formed sinks and washbasins are available, as well as worktops and counters with or without inset drainage grooves.

• Long-lasting. Worn Corian fixtures can be removed, repolished and reinstalled.

• Translucent in some colours and in thinner sections.

Applications

• Kitchen counters and worktops with or without integral drainage grooves or integral splashbacks.

• Sinks and washbasins.

• Vanity tops.

• Vertical cladding.

Finish

• Corian has a satin sheen finish that becomes silkier with use.

3

4

5

The lustre will develop evenly if the surface is cleaned according to the manufacturer's guidance.
• Routine cleaning is generally enough to keep it looking good. Tackle spills immediately.
• Although heat-resistant, Corian can scorch if you set a hot pan on it and will discolour if you pour boiling water on it.
• Never cut or chop directly on the surface.

• Chemical spills, burn marks, scratches or resistant stains can be sanded off in situ.

Composite stone

Composite stone is a manufactured material made from quartz bound with resin. It is worked like stone but delivers a number of practical benefits and is generally much cheaper. It comes in different thicknesses and edge profiles and can be used for kitchen and bathroom worktops, fire surrounds and mantelpieces.

Characteristics
• Impervious to water.
• Huge vibrant colour range.
• Exceptional heat-resistance.
• Scratch- and stain-resistant.
• Long-lasting.
• Needs professional installation.

Applications
• As for Corian.

Finish
• Composite stone needs no further finishing and can be simply wiped clean.

1. A wall-mounted Corian sink.
2. Rectangular Corian washbasins in vivid colours.
3. Corian worktop with inset drainage grooves.
4. Pristine composite stone used to clad a kitchen island.
5. Corian can be very finely detailed.

1

2

3

4

decorative laminate

One of the most common composite materials in domestic use is laminate, widely used for kitchen counters and bathroom vanity tops. High-pressure decorative laminate is composed of layers of paper impregnated with thermosetting synthetic resins bonded under pressure and heat. The material contains up to 60 per cent paper. Thermosets are a type of plastic that become soft and malleable when heated, but once they have set, remain rigid and cannot be softened again. They are stronger and have better fire-resistance than thermoplastics.

The leading brand name in the field is Formica®, which again has become a generic term for this type of surfacing material. Formica has been manufactured since the mid-1940s and early examples, on tabletops for instance, have retro appeal. A black edge is characteristic, though a through-coloured version of the material is available.

Characteristics
• Although a considerable proportion of decorative laminates on the market are designed to simulate wood and other natural finishes, the material is also available in an enormous range of colours and patterns, including metallics.
• Grades vary, from panels designed for light use to more robust materials of higher performance. The highest grades of laminate are strong, dimensionally stable, fire-retardant and can be cut and worked into different shapes.
• High-grade laminates are wear-, moisture- and impact-resistant.
• Some types of laminate are through-coloured.
• Hygienic and low maintenance.
• Poor-quality laminate is not as wear-resistant and the surface can delaminate over time. Using the wrong grade in areas subject to humidity or heavy wear can also cause the material to degrade.
• Large panel sizes are available for economic coverage.

Applications
• Kitchen worktops, counters and splashbacks, shelving and tabletops. Choose the grades suitable for horizontal use.
• Bathroom vanity tops. A special version of Formica is produced for shower cubicles. Choose moisture-resistant types.
• Built-in workstations and shelving.
• Wall cladding. Veneers and other laminates designed to be used vertically are less hardwearing. Generally fixed to timber battens or glued to a prepared surface lined with plywood or hardboard.
• Doors.
• It is recommended to store laminate in the conditions in which it will be installed for a few days beforehand to let it acclimatize. Allow air to reach the backs of the panels as well as the fronts.

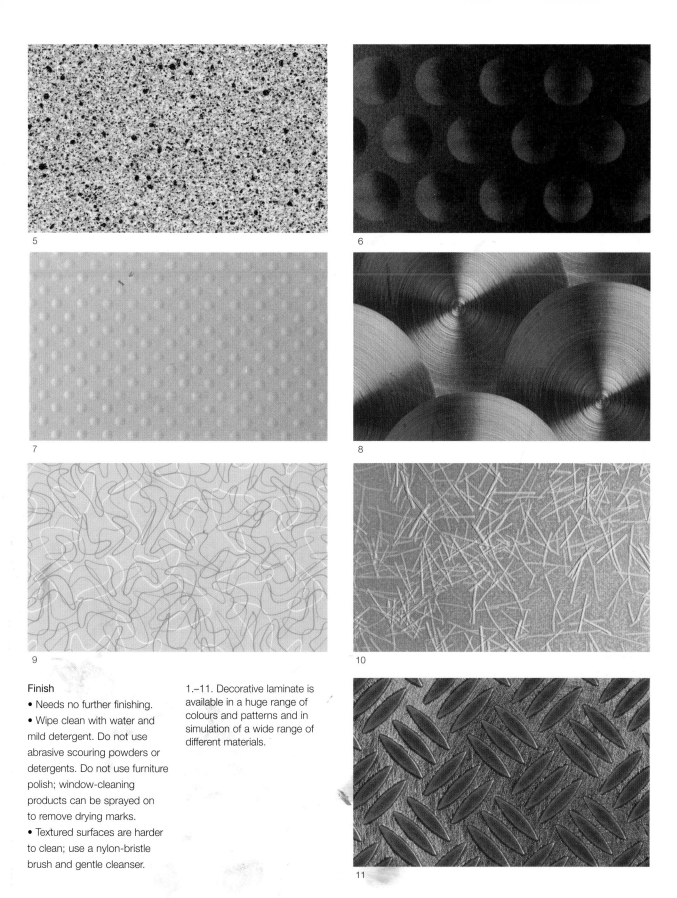

5

6

7

8

9

10

Finish
• Needs no further finishing.
• Wipe clean with water and mild detergent. Do not use abrasive scouring powders or detergents. Do not use furniture polish; window-cleaning products can be sprayed on to remove drying marks.
• Textured surfaces are harder to clean; use a nylon-bristle brush and gentle cleanser.

1.–11. Decorative laminate is available in a huge range of colours and patterns and in simulation of a wide range of different materials.

11

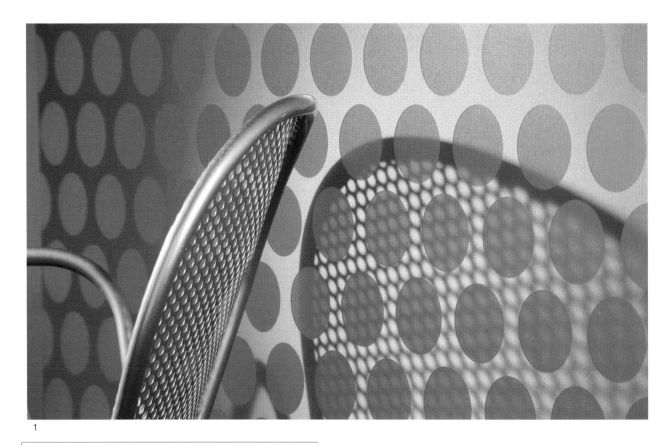

1

sheet resin

A particularly expressive family of products, panels and sheets formed of cast resin provide the vehicle for decorative interlayers as well as luminous glowing colour. While the basic ingredient is synthetic resin, which places the material squarely in the nonnatural camp, one company manufactures a panel range from 100 per cent recycled post-consumer HDPE (high density polythene) reprocessed and recoloured, giving it excellent green credentials.

The translucency of these panels means that they are particularly effective when backlit, either by artificial lighting or by natural light. Depending on application and size, they can be installed and supported in a variety of ways: from cables, rails or rods, in frameworks or in sliding channels.

Characteristics
• Beguiling design and decorative possibilities. Patterning may be random and abstract or delivered by textiles or thin three-dimensional objects, such as grasses, fossil leaves and petals, used as interlayers.
• Translucent, with clear or frosted finishes.
• Can be worked by standard woodworking tools.
• Can be lit from either the back or the front.
• Available in a range of sizes and in a standard thickness of just under 2cm, but custom fabrications are also possible.
• Products containing recycled plastic are environmentally friendly.
• Flammable.

Applications
• As vertical elements in the interior – doors, partitions, dividers, feature walls and cladding.
• As horizontal elements – shelving, counters and tabletops.

Finish
• No further finishing is required.
• Repolishing and cleaning can be achieved with nonabrasive household cleansers.
• Like any plastics-based material, the surface is degraded by scratching.

1. Sheet resin with a frosted spot pattern.
2. Sheet resin with a seedhead interlayer.
3. Sheet resin with an interlayer of dried grasses.
4. Depending on the interlayer, panels can be more or less translucent.

2

3

4

rubber

One of the legacies of high-tech was the adoption of rubber as a floor covering in domestic interiors. In the 1980s, when rubber was chiefly familiar as a robust flooring in stations, airports, hospitals and other heavy-traffic contexts, it had a no-nonsense utilitarian quality and the colour range was accordingly limited to neutrals with the odd primary shade. As it has become more popular in contemporary homes, the colour range has exploded to include some 70 vibrant shades, as well as terrazzo and marbled patterning. Another plus is unbeatable practical performance across the board.

Most rubber flooring is virtually wholly synthetic, made of SBR rubber, a petrochemical derivative. But a new generation of rubber is now available, which is up to 90 per cent natural in origin. While it is possible to apply rubber to vertical surfaces as a wall finish, the overwhelming application is as flooring.

Although rubber tiles are manageable and easy to handle, professional installation gives the best result. The subfloor must be dry, even, clean and porous. A smoothing or levelling compound is best applied to concrete floors; for timber floors a covering of 6mm-thick plywood is recommended. Adhesive is applied to both the subfloor and the tiles, and the two surfaces are brought together after a specified period.

After installation, the floor should be swept clean and any excess adhesive removed. No wet cleaning should take place for a week until the adhesive has fully cured. Sealing with a specialist dressing is recommended after installation. Relief-textured rubber may collect more dirt and can be harder to keep clean.

Opposite: A seamless expanse of glossy rubber flooring.

Formats
• Most rubber is sold in the form of tiles of various thicknesses. A thickness of 2.5mm is recommended for domestic floors; thicknesses of up to 4mm are also produced for areas of heavy traffic.
• Standard tile dimensions are 680 x 680mm.
• For a more seamless look, it is possible to source larger tiles of the sort that are used as station flooring, but colours are limited.
• Rubber is also available in sheet form, but it is heavy and unwieldy to install in this format.
• Specialist installation is recommended. The success of a rubber floor depends on the proper preparation of the subfloor and the use of specialist adhesive.

Characteristics
• Soft, warm and tactile. Although rubber is incredibly tough, it feels comfortable underfoot.
• Dimensionally stable. Rubber will not shrink or expand and there is no need for seam welding.
• Huge colour range. Colours remain fast and are resistant to fading.
• Nonslip textural surfaces include studded, ridged, treadplate, gridded and pebbled.
• Patterns include marbled and terrazzo designs. One company allows you to design your own patterns by specifying colours and chip shape.
• Cutting services are available to create inlay designs.
• Rubber tiles suitable for outdoor use come in a range of muted natural colours.
• Rubber resists acid and cigarette burns. It is very durable and long-lasting.
• Can be used over underfloor heating.
• Antistatic, antislip and antibacterial.
• Withstands scuffing and reduces noise.

Applications
• As flooring. Relief textures minimize slipping in areas likely to become wet, such as bathrooms.
• Rubber designed for outdoor use can be used around swimming pools, on balconies and roof gardens, on decks, terraces and paths.
• Rubber can be used on stairs and landings provided there are substantial nosings to prevent slipping.

1

3

2

natural rubber

Relatively new on the market is a rubber tile that is 90 per cent natural in composition, enhancing the material's environmental credentials. Natural rubber is a wholly renewable resource and mature rubber trees have been shown to be particularly efficient at absorbing carbon dioxide from the atmosphere. The production of rubber has none of the adverse environmental impacts associated with the petrochemical industry.

Further advantages from a green point of view is that all types of rubber, including synthetic, are easy to recycle, not merely once, but over and over. Added to which, rubber has a low toxicity compared with PVC (the constituent of vinyl flooring) as well as an incredibly long life.

Natural rubber shares the same characteristics as synthetic and is available in a similar range of colours and textures. It is suitable for the same applications and is installed and maintained in the same way. Eco rubber, another product made from recycled rubber, shows some colour variation from tile to tile.

1. Vibrant colour is a particular feature of rubber flooring.
2. Colour and pattern ranges are vast.
3. Rubber flooring with a sanded texture, suitable for external use.
4. Marbled finish.
5. Relief patterning.
6. Studded rubber.
7. Flecked design.

4

5

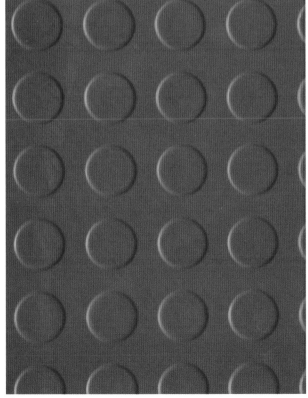

6

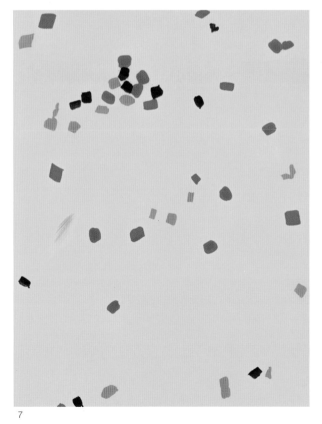

7

poured resin

Mistakenly and popularly known as 'poured rubber', poured resin makes an exceptionally glossy and stylish floor. Developed as a hardwearing coating for industrial and commercial applications, it has in recent years been seen in domestic interiors, too, particularly on a larger scale – where the layout is sweeping and open-plan, for example, or in lofts and other converted spaces. Its chief drawback is the difficulty of installation and it is not unknown for it to take several attempts before the floor cures and sets properly.

Various formulations are available, depending on the performance required, but the basic ingredient is some form of synthetic resin. Synthetic resins fall under the category of thermosetting plastics; epoxy resin is one example.

Characteristics

• Integral seam-free finish that is very durable and hardwearing.
• Different finishes are available from high gloss to matt. Some types incorporate decorative flakes for added sparkle. Others result in a marbled appearance similar to polished concrete. Semi-transparent resins have great depth and a certain three-dimensional quality.
• Good colour range.
• Thicknesses vary from around 2mm to 5mm, according to product formulation.
• Warm feel underfoot, with sound-deadening qualities. Slightly flexible.
• Moderately slip-resistant, particularly in the matt finishes.
• Odour-free products are available. Some resins are designed to be fast-curing.
• Lighter floors show scuff marks. Certain chemicals will dull or discolour the floor.

Applications

• Flooring, particularly larger surface areas.

Installation

• Requires specialist installation by a professional who has experience in this type of work.
• The subfloor should be concrete, structurally sound, stable and free from contamination by any chemical that could affect the penetration of the primer.
• Special products are available for jointing.
• Installation must be carried out within a recommended temperature range to ensure proper curing.
• The resin base and hardener is mixed in measured amounts on site and applied using a brush or a lambswool roller.
• Curing times vary according to the formulation. Some additional protection in the form of a removable covering may be needed until the floor is fully hardened.

Finish

• No subsequent finishing is required.
• Vacuum or sweep loose dirt.
• Wash with a recommended cleanser and rinse well.

Opposite: The height of contemporary chic, a poured-resin floor is light-enhancing and luxurious-looking.

tiles

The tile is a convenient humanly scaled format for cladding walls, floors and other surfaces in a variety of materials – hard, soft and somewhere in between. The most popular and most widely available remains the ceramic tile.

Ceramic tiles in plain or neutral shades make understated hardworking backdrops in clean-lined contemporary interiors, particularly when they are used to cover entire surfaces. These types of hard tiles are wear-, stain- and water-resistant, which makes them appropriate for areas such as kitchens and bathrooms. Very smooth versions, however, are best not used on floors where they will be too slippery when wet. A particular feature of a ceramic tiled surface is the graphic gridded pattern it makes, which in turn is a function of the size of the tile and the degree at which individual tiles are spaced. Most tiles are glued or embedded in position leaving a narrow margin on all sides, which is subsequently filled by grouting. (See also pages 64–5).

In the contemporary interior the range of tiles extends beyond ceramic to embrace other materials, such as leather, pebbles and glass, each with their own aesthetic and practical characteristics. When industrial or commercial materials were first introduced into the domestic interior and used to cover large surface areas, installation was not always straightforward. The tile format changes all that. Metal tiles, for example (see pages 116–19), deliver a crisp, modern aesthetic in a manageable way.

Decoratively speaking, the advent of digital technology has also given the standard ceramic tile a whole new dimension. Digital patterns and motifs transcend the standardized format and open up exciting creative possibilities. On this level, an element of handmaking and custom design comes into the picture, elevating the humble tile to a showstopper in its own right.

Characteristics

• Chiefly defined by the manageable format that allows large surfaces to be covered without the need to manoeuvre unwieldy sheets into place.
• Tiles are available in an ever expanding range of materials, from hard products made of ceramic, terracotta and the like, right through to softer leather, vinyl and lino.
• Tiles are also available in the form of mesh-backed sheets that allow small elements such as mosaic or pebbles to be easily installed.
• Maintenance and installation is largely a factor of the material itself. Different adhesives are recommended for different products.
• Even tiles when laid form a grid pattern that can be accentuated by the colour and breadth of grouting. Other tile formats, such as pebble tiles, are interlocking to produce an integral surface.

Opposite: Glass wall tiles introduce a rhythmic quality.

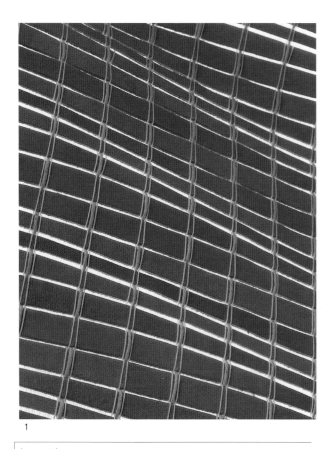

1

2

leather

Leather is a supremely luxurious finishing material. Most familiar in the interior as a covering for furniture, it is now available as tiles that can be used to clad walls and floors. One of the beauties of leather is its evocative smell; its warm, supple texture also invites touch – walking barefoot on a leather floor is a uniquely tactile experience. Like any natural material, leather improves with age. Scratching is inevitable when it is used in a flooring application, but the patina of use adds to its charm, just as leather upholstery that has seen a bit of wear can also be very appealing.

The leather that is used for flooring is more robust than upholstery leather. It is made from top-quality bison hide, cut from the central portion where the fibres are strongest and where the hide is uniformly thick. The leather is then slowly cured in drums using vegetable tanning and coloured with aniline dyes.

Characteristics

• A warm, sensuous material that gives an interior a quality of bespoke elegance.
• Available in a range of colours, from rich natural shades, such as brown and russet, to reds, greens, blues and black. Subtle patterning can be created by mixing light and dark tiles to give a chequered effect.
• Because it is a wholly natural material, variation may occur from tile to tile.

• Wall tiles are treated on the back to facilitate gluing and prevent shrinkage or expansion due to temperature change. Edges may be dyed. Tiles are laser-cut to size.
• Floor tiles consist of a 3mm leather square bonded to an 11mm wooden backing with tongue-and-groove joints. Marine ply can be specified as the backing for damper locations. Various sizes between 20 x 20cm and 50 x 50cm are available.
• Flame-retardant tiles can be specified.

Applications

• To clad walls and other vertical surfaces.
• As flooring. Apply over a perfectly smooth, even subfloor. Section bars glued into the grooves of the tiles align each row and create a tightly bonded unit. A day after laying, the tiles can be walked on.

Finish

• Maintenance wax rubbed into the leather after it is installed seals the joints and prevents moisture penetration.
• Leather floors should be maintained in the same way as hardwood floors.

1. Leather can be used for upholstery, wall cladding and even flooring.
2. Woven leather mats.
3. Leather chair on leather floor tiles.

3

1

2

photoceramics & digital tiles

With the advent of digital technology, surface patterning has taken a new twist. Tiles have long been the vehicle for decoration and textural effects. Photorealist tiles are the most recent manifestation of the tile's inherent aesthetic versatility.

In recent years, digital print technology has become more and more sophisticated and new digital tiles have good tonal values, colour saturation, detail and durability – unlike those novelty products (mugs printed with family snapshots, for example) where the image fades with time and use. The decorative scope is limitless. Photographic images may be printed on tiles as single motifs – like hand-painted decoration. An image may be blown up and printed over a large number of tiles to form a tiled mural. Or photographic imagery can be used to create abstract patterning, a modern version of traditional Moorish designs. Some examples of digital tilework include a shower cubicle tiled with a rainforest scene, a bathroom floor where you 'walk on water' and a blue sky with fluffy white clouds that forms a kitchen splashback – *trompe l'oeil* for the modern age.

Sources of imagery

• Digital tile producers generally have standard images to choose from and may also have contractual relationships with photo libraries.
• A number of artists and designers are also working in this field, some in association with tile producers.
• You can provide a tile producer with your own image on CD or by email. The better the original image quality, the better the reproduction.
• Any printed image can be scanned and transferred to tile – graphics, maps, posters, diagrams and so on.

Characteristics

• Available as floor and wall tiles in a range of sizes. Floor tiles are either ceramic or quartz (suitable for heavy traffic).
• Tiles are fired and glazed at high temperatures and are hardwearing. They will not fade or degrade.
• Matt, satin or gloss finishes are available.

• Tile murals are numbered individually and are supplied with a map for installation.
• Priced according to quantity, size and image; minimum orders generally apply and production time may be up to six weeks.
• Installed and maintained in the same way as other ceramic tiles.

Applications

• On walls as splashbacks, in bathrooms and shower cubicles.
• On floors.
• Tiles can be ordered that are suitable for exterior use.

Finish

• No subsequent finishing is necessary.
• Clean with the same grout cleansers as standard tiles.

1.–8. A vibrant range of digitally
printed ceramic tiles.

1

functional tiles

Contemporary variants on the tile format are the 'Functional', 'Construction' and 'Kitchen' tiles designed by the Dutch group Droog. Tiling hardworking areas such as kitchens and bathrooms generally means cutting tiles to fit around fixtures such as taps, or drilling into tiles to fix such details as hooks and toilet-roll holders in place. It can be fiddly work and the result is not always as seamless as one would hope. Droog's witty designs incorporate such features as part of the tile itself.

Integrated functions include egg timers, mortars and hanging racks in the kitchen range and toilet-paper holders, towel hooks and a small medicine chest in the bathroom.

Three-dimensional solutions for corners and edges, such as convex or concave tiles, mean that rooms can be completely tiled without awkward cutting or visual interruptions to the tiling grid. Another series of kitchen tiles feature integral gas burners and control switches.

Characteristics
• Witty three-dimensional tile designs that combine function with sculptural effect.
• White glazed ceramic with surface relief.
• Waterproof.
• Installed like any other ceramic tile.
• Designs are based around the standard 15 x 15cm format, which means that plain tiles can be combined with

2

special functional tiles for a custom result.

Applications
• Wall cladding in kitchens and bathrooms.

Finish
• No subsequent finishing required.
• Clean and maintain as for standard tiles.

1. Ventilation-grid tile.
2. Toilet-paper dispenser tile.
3. Towel hook tile.
4. Cube tiles to make bathroom ledges.

3

4

1

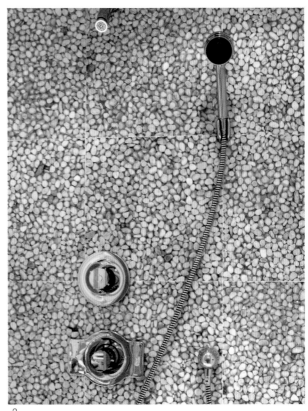

2

pebble tiles

Pebbles and cobbles – small loose stones rounded by time, weather or water – have a long history of domestic use, either loosely heaped to make garden paths and borders or embedded in mortar to make the type of decorative mosaics that are a traditional feature of Mediterranean houses and courtyards. Today mesh-backed pebble tiles vastly simplify installation and broaden the applications enormously, both indoors and out. These can be used for flooring, in shower rooms, as wall cladding, as kitchen splashbacks, as fire surrounds and pool surrounds, and in countless other applications.

Variations on this theme are interlocking mesh-backed wall tiles composed of random fragments of stone arranged as crazy paving, in stacking blocks, in undulating wave formations or in linear slivers. Another product consists of riverbed pebbles encased in transparent resin to form smooth panels that can be used on floors, on walls and in water features.

Characteristics
• Durable and hardwearing.
• Wide range of colour, stone type and size. Smaller pebbles are best suited to vertical surfaces. Stones are sorted for size and colour before being made into tiles.
• Tiles are available in squares, interlocking on all sides so that there are no visible joints.

3

• Standing pebble tiles have a more pronounced texture. Pebbles are cut in half and set standing for a highly contoured surface.
• Riverstone panels come in three colours (red, blue and green) and three pebble sizes. Thicknesses are 10mm, 14mm and 22mm up to a maximum dimension of 80 x 180cm. Sunlight can cause the resin

to change colour so these products are best used indoors.

Applications
• The range of applications is wide, as with any weatherproof tile. Tiles featuring small pebbles can be curved around columns and other curved features.
• Tiles should be sorted and dry-laid before installation to ensure an even colour layout.

4

5

6

7

• Installation is by adhesive, over a flat, clean, dry substrate. A waterproof membrane is recommended in wet areas. For flooring, a fall of 4cm to a drainage point is required. Movement joints need to be incorporated if the surface is large or there are likely to be extreme temperature and humidity variations.

Finish

• Tiles should be sealed before and after grouting. Pre-sealing enables grout splashes to be removed more easily. The pre-sealer must be compatible with the final seal.

• Riverstone panels are polished with marble wax.

1. Mesh-backed pebble tiles used in a shower room.
2. Detail of pebble tiles.
3. Different sizes of pebble and stone are used.
4.–5. Some pebble tiles are interlocking so that there are no visible joints.
6.–7. Flat stone tiles are suitable for vertical surfaces.

1

2

glass tiles

In the case of glass, the tile format translates a material that is heavy, unwieldy and prone to shatter into a much more manageable form. Glass tiling has a luminous quality that gives depth to surfaces and finishes, especially in transparent or translucent versions.

Types of glass tile

• The most common type of glass tile is glass mosaic, small individual tiles about 2cm square mesh-backed to create sheets 30 x 30cm for ease of installation.

• More recently, large-format glass tiles have been produced, some of which can be used on the floor. Individual glass tiles are produced in a range of shapes and dimensions up to 30 x 30cm.

Glass and ceramic

Like oil and water, glass and ceramic naturally repel each other. A recent innovation is the 'Drop Tile', produced for Droog as part of its 'Dry Bathing Project', after research was undertaken to find a type of glass that would stick to ceramic. Pieces of glass are placed on the tiles by hand before they go into the kiln. The glass liquefies in the kiln and fuses with the ceramic during cooling, so that the surface looks as if it is covered with drops of water. The bubbled texture has a massaging effect and is nonslip, so tiles can be used on the floor as well as the walls. No two tiles are alike.

Characteristics

• Huge range of colours. Finishes include clear, translucent, opalescent, tumbled and frosted.

• Mosaic is available in random and repeating patterns and as mesh-backed panels of glass pebbles for a more rustic look.

• Impervious to liquids and vapours.

• Resists fading, staining and discolouration.

• Chips, scratches and cracks easily. Must not be exposed to thermal shock or impact.

• Can be used externally or internally, in wet or dry locations.

• Cannot be installed over flexible surfaces.

• Recycled glass tiles are available in chunkier and less regular shapes.

Applications

• As wall cladding in kitchens and bathrooms; as decorative borders and feature tiles.

• On counters.

• Flooring. Installing glass tiles requires more care than installing ceramic tiles. It is often recommended to apply over a crack-suppression membrane, particularly if there is a risk that the subfloor will shrink or move after installation. Use only matt-textured glass tiles on floors and never in areas that are likely to become wet.

Finish

• No subsequent sealing is required in normal use. Where tiles are used on counters, a tile sealer is recommended to make cleaning easier.

3

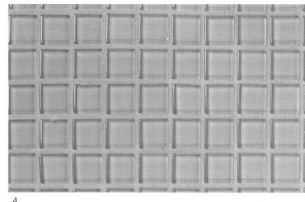

4

5

6

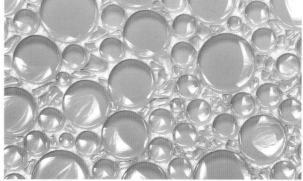

7

• Clean with nonabrasive
cleansers and rinse carefully.
Any glass surface requires
more maintenance to stay
looking good.

1. Glass mosaic wall in
a bathroom.
2. Diagonal glass tiles.
3. Larger-format square
glass tiles.
4.–6. Glass mosaic.
7.–8. Glass bead tiles.

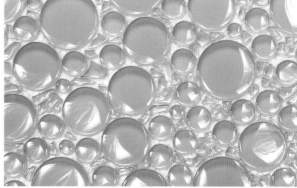

8

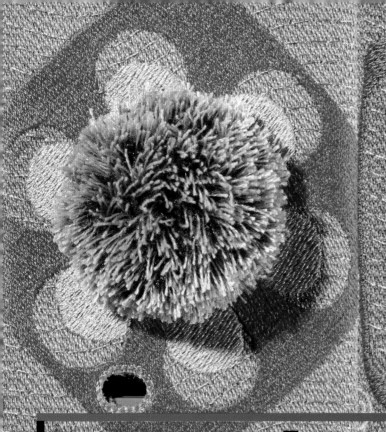

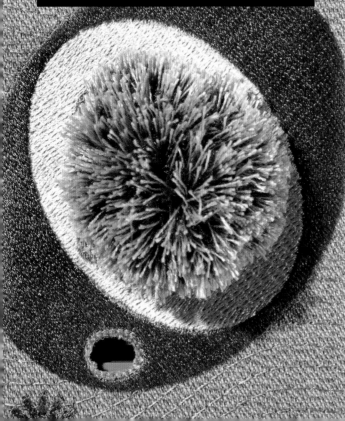

smart

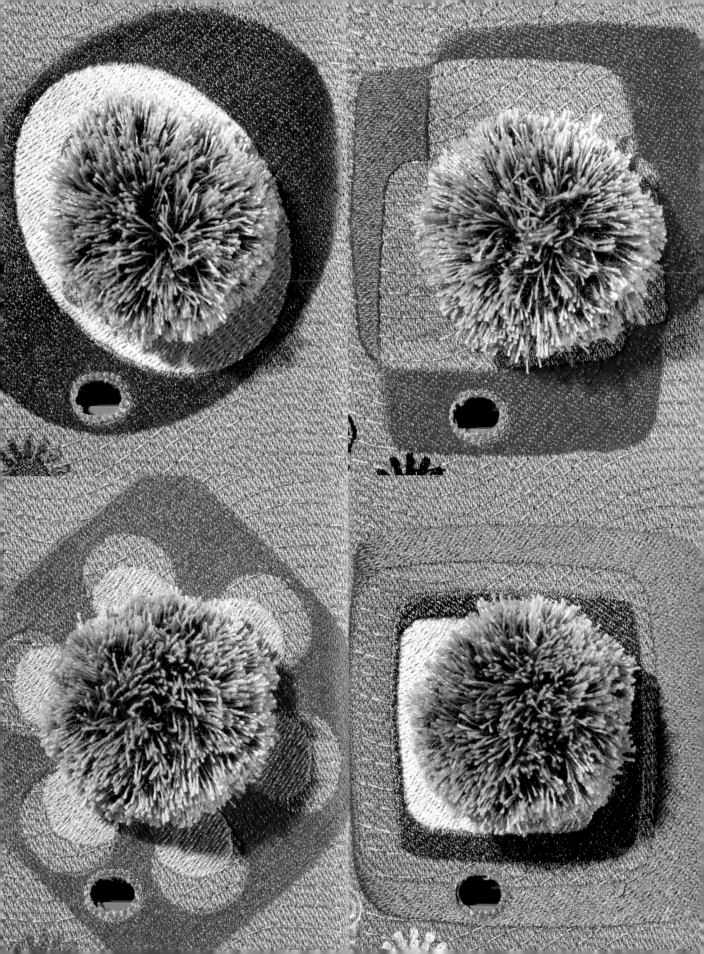

smart
introduction

Smart materials are shape-shifters of form and function, challenging our notions of what a material can be. Advances in technology have brought us glass that can be switched from opaque to transparent and back again, wallpaper that reacts to changes in temperature, and electroluminescent fabric that brightens and darkens according to ambient light levels. Is a tile studded with LEDs primarily a surface covering or a light? This blurring of roles both inspires wonder and introduces a playful element to the interior. In some cases, the technology has been around for a while, but it has taken a certain vision to interpret it in new and exciting ways. It is far from surprising that many of the most intriguing applications have been created by artist-makers experimenting with new techniques on the cutting edge of design.

Materials that interact with their surroundings make the inanimate come alive. Many of the examples featured in this section explore the medium of light in such a way that light itself almost becomes a material. Others turn our expectations upside down – a tile that can be repositioned whenever and wherever you want redefines the solid world.

While most of the materials in this section are in mainstream production, some are not. Many new materials or applications of material technology first see the light of day as projects, prototypes or one-off installations and take time to become more widely available. Inevitably, this means that selection may not be as straightforward as sourcing more standard materials – you may have to make a custom order, wait for it to be fulfilled and be prepared for the fact that there will not necessarily be a body of knowledge out there to assist in installation and maintenance. At the same time, this is a period when the pace of materials technology is advancing at quite a rate and what can seem positively futuristic one moment might well have the potential to become almost commonplace before you know it.

Above: Electroluminescent 'Light Sleeper' bedding reacts
to changing light levels.

reactive glass

We are using more and more glass in our homes and public buildings, creating structures that are light and airy and that animate the interior with clear views of the world outside. In turn, this demand has driven many significant advances in glass technology in recent years that address not only certain practical disadvantages of the material, but also usher in the potential for its redefinition.

Little under a century ago, a house with glass walls was revolutionary in itself. With the arrival of reactive glass, those walls can be transformed into smart skins that mediate the interior both physically and visually. Naturally enough, these new types of glass have been designed primarily with commercial applications in mind – for example, displays, signage, demonstrations and presentations achieve greater clarity and impact using back projection onto liquid crystal windows. But architects and designers are also introducing such materials in domestic settings, too, and perhaps one day the idea of a window that doesn't do something will seem positively quaint.

The basic principle behind many smart windows, particularly the switchable ones, is more or less the same. However, they are manufactured in different ways, which affects their light-blocking properties and, to a lesser extent, their visual appearance.

Characteristics
• Encompasses a range of products that react in some way to their environment, either for practical reasons (self-cleaning glass) or for more aesthetic purposes.
• Some forms of reactive glass reduce glare and reflection and can be used as part of an energy-saving strategy.
• Relatively expensive. Some types are at an early stage of development and availability may be limited.
• Technical advice should be sought for specification and installation.
• Maintenance is generally straightforward and similar to that for standard glass.

Opposite: Switchable glazing goes from transparent to opaque at the touch of a button.

liquid crystal glazing

Glass has always been valued for its transparency, but there are times when we don't want to be exposed to view. Screening windows with blinds or curtains is the low-tech option. Installing translucent or obscured glass is an alternative. Glazing that turns from translucent to clear at the flick of a switch offers the best of both worlds. In the obscured or translucent setting, light is still allowed through.

Liquid crystal glass is a laminated product. The inner core is a layer of tiny liquid crystals. Sandwiching that are two interlayers of film, whose inner faces are covered with a transparent electrically conductive metal coating. The outer layers are glass sheet. The conductive coatings are connected to a flat electrical busbar fixed on one of the glass edges, which in turn connects the glass to a power supply. When the power is off, the liquid crystals are randomly scattered, diffusing light in all directions, and the glazing is translucent and milky white. When the glazing is switched on, the crystals align and allow light through. The liquid crystals in switchable glass, technically known as PDLCs (polymer-dispersed liquid crystals) share technical similarities with LCDs (liquid crystal displays).

Characteristics

• Instantaneous switching from translucent (off) to clear (on). Switching can be repeated as desired or programmed to switch continuously. Must be left off for at least four hours a day.
• Allows virtually the same amount of light through in either setting, particularly in the extra-white glass specification.
• Provides security and privacy on demand.
• Clear, bronze, grey or green.
• Can be curved, silkscreen-printed or sandblasted.
• Can be used as single or double glazing, safety glazing and insulating glazing.
• Excellent for back projections.
• Good soundproofing.
• Hygienic.
• Relatively expensive.
• Available in thicknesses from 7mm to 14mm and in a number of shapes. Nonavailable shapes include those without a straight edge, and shapes that are notched or pierced.
• Maximum size is 3,000 x 2,000mm. Larger expanses can be achieved by using panels side by side. Joints are filled with transparent silicone seal.
• Can be made from polycarbonate as well as glass.
• No in-between settings – glass is clear or translucent.
• Requires power to be transparent, though only a small amount. Does not reduce light or energy levels so it is not energy-efficient used on its own.

Applications

• Chiefly internal. The glazing can be used as an element of external glazing if it forms the inner pane in a double-glazing unit. Technical advice is required.
• Internal doors (including sliding doors), partitions and openings.
• Can be used in floor tiles.
• Not suitable for roof glazing.

Finish

• No subsequent finishing.
• Maintain as for standard glass.

1

SPD glazing

Another variant on the smart-window theme is SPD (suspended particle device) glazing. The technology is similar to that used in liquid crystal glazing. Light-absorbing microscopic particles are dispersed in a thin film encased in glass. When power is applied, the particles align and allow light through. When power is switched off, the particles absorb light and the glass is dark.

The chief advantage of SPD glazing over liquid crystal glazing is that it can be used to control light levels to a precise degree and thus is capable of playing an active role in energy-saving strategies. Use of this and similar types of glass has the potential to reduce energy needs by 20 to 30 per cent. Although the technology is developed, its take-up by glazing manufacturers is currently at an early stage.

1.–3. Liquid crystal glazing used to screen a bathroom from a bedroom. When switched off, the glass is translucent.

2

3

electrochromic glazing

The third principal type of switchable glass is electrochromic glazing. Like the others, it consists of glass panes sandwiching several interlayers. However, it works rather differently from either liquid crystal glass or SPD glass. A low voltage is passed across microscopically thin coatings on the glass surface, activating a tungsten-bearing electrochromic layer and causing it to change colour from clear to a darker blue.

Characteristics
• Darkening of the glass reduces glare and reflection and avoids overheating.
• Avoids the need for external shades.
• Glass lightens when sunlight is low, reducing the need for artificial light.
• Trials have shown that such glass can reduce the energy required for air conditioning by half.
• Coating on the glass helps keep heat in during winter.
• Power can be operated manually or by sensors responding to light intensity.
• Power is required only to change opacity, not to maintain a given shade.
• Responds slowly, with the colour change beginning at the outer edge of the window and moving towards the centre.

Applications
• Potentially wide use in external glazing.

holographic glass

The same principle that creates shimmering colours on certain butterfly and hummingbird wings has been applied to create glass that appears to change colour according to where you are in relation to it. This is due to a holographic grid, sandwiched between laminated foil and clear glass layers. Holographic grids or gratings split ambient white light into a full spectrum. Depending on where you stand, you will see either clear glass or a different band of colour.

One of the benefits of this type of glazing is saving energy. As roof glazing, it can redirect light into parts of the interior that would otherwise be dark. As external glazing, it can refract light into deep rooms or form part of a sun-protection strategy on south-facing elevations.

Holographic glass has been used commercially to accent façades and entrances. In a domestic setting, it could be effective in smaller applications such as internal partitions.

Characteristics
• Glass that looks clear until you reach the angle of refraction.
• Decorative wash of rainbow shades that shift as you move.
• Can be incorporated into all sorts of glass, including curved.
• Energy-saving.
• Improves natural daylighting in otherwise underlit areas.
• The effect is not reversible.

Applications
• External glazing, roof glazing, internal partitions and displays.

1

self-cleaning glass

Keeping glass in pristine condition traditionally involves the expenditure of plenty of elbow grease – or the services of a window cleaner. As we use more glass in our homes, in greater quantities and in locations that may be difficult to reach, cleaning becomes a greater practical issue. Glazed extensions and glazed roofs quickly lose their appeal when they become streaked with dirt and less than crystal-clear.

Self-cleaning glass is glass with a special coating that destroys organic dirt. During manufacture, a thin film of titanium dioxide 15 nanometres thick is applied to the glass in a process called chemical vapour deposition. This coating requires daylight and rainwater to work effectively and is thus for external use only. In chemical reaction with UV rays, the coating loosens and breaks down organic dirt into carbon dioxide and water vapour. It also reduces the surface tension of water so that it runs off and washes the dirt away rather than forming droplets.

Characteristics
• Keeps glass free from organic dirt, saving time and money. Safer than cleaning windows yourself, particularly those that can be reached only by ladders, such as upper-floor windows, conservatory roofs and other sloping roofs.
• Appearance is clearer than standard glass.
• The coating cannot be worn away and lasts the lifetime of the glass.
• Available in clear and blue-tinted versions and in different thicknesses.
• Requires specialist sealants that do not leach silicone – silicone damages the coating.
• Can be used in combination with other forms of glazing according to required performance: for example, with glass designed for thermal insulation, security or noise control. It can be toughened or laminated. As part of a glazed unit, it should be used as the outer pane.
• Antibacterial. Prevents fungi and mould growth.
• Cannot be sandblasted.
• About 20 per cent more expensive than standard glass.

Applications
• All types of external glazing, particularly those that are inaccessible.
• Self-cleaning glass needs daylight and rainfall to work. Glazed roofs should slope to encourage water runoff.
• Technical advice is recommended for framing and suitable sealants.

Finish
• No subsequent finishing.
• Maintenance is low. However, during dry periods the glass may need hosing down to simulate the action of rainfall. Alternatively, it can be cleaned with a soft cloth and soapy water.
• Avoid touching the glass as fingerprints may cause inorganic dirt to adhere.

2

Similarly, gloves should be worn during installation to prevent damaging the coating or contaminating it in some way.
• The glass requires several days of exposure to daylight before becoming active and should not be touched during this time.

1. Self-cleaning glass window walls keep the view pristine.
2. Little maintenance is required.
3. Self-cleaning glass is ideal where glazing is hard to reach.

3

tiles

Everyone knows what a tile is – a unit of some type of solid material scaled to the hand and applied to walls, floors and other surfaces in multiples. Yet technology is redefining this familiar decorative element, too, creating products that call into question our most basic assumptions. Tiles that are soft, squidgy and removable, or ones that glow with light when pressed, take a familiar format into uncharted territory.

Characteristics

• Smart tiles share the same manageable hand-scaled format as conventional tiles.

• Smart tiles range from beguilingly simple interactive products to those that have had sophisticated technological input.

• Smart tiles generally do something – they light up, can be repositioned or glow in the dark.

• Specification varies according to product, as does maintenance and installation.

• Some of these products are still at prototype stage or form part of a one-off design/art project.

Opposite: LED floor tiles arranged in a strip.

1

repositionable gel tiles

Most tiles, once applied to a surface, are there for the duration, as the strong adhesives used to stick them in place tend to rule out frequent redecoration. For the same reason, they require a certain degree of precision to install: imperfect tilework is always an eyesore.

An original application of a material developed in the plastics industry, 'Jelly Tile', by Japanese designer Keiko Oyabu, is made of polyurethane gel, which means that it can be easily removed and rearranged. Unlike most tiles, which tend to be made of hard materials, gel tiles are soft, squeezable and come in degrees of transparency, which makes them ideally suited for use with other transparent surfaces, such as glass, or in combination with lighting. A fun material that brings lively, tactile qualities into play, these tiles achieve a degree of practicality in bathrooms where they make cold, smooth surfaces softer, safer and more comfortable.

Characteristics

• Soft, pliable and cushioning.
• The backs of the tiles are self-adhesive, which means that they can be applied and reapplied many times to create different patterns, or moved from place to place.
• Satin finish. Available in a range of colours and in degrees of transparency from clear to translucent.
• Water- and heat-resistant.

• Resilient and moderately noise-reducing.
• Scratch-resistant.
• Nonrenewable.
• Available in plain colours, in an undulating wave pattern and shaped like a rose. The format is 125 x 125 x 11mm, but the tiles can be easily cut to smaller dimensions. The rose tile is also available in a square format measuring 450 x 450 x 20mm.

Applications

• Apply to any smooth, clean surface such as glass, metal or glazed ceramic.
• Makes a cushioning, comfortable finish when applied in a shower cubicle.

Finish

• Requires no further finish.
• When the adhesive quality or sheen begins to wear off, the tiles can be restored simply by immersing them in warm water and drying them.

1. Large-format 'Jelly Tile' with a rose motif.
2. Tiles are self-adhesive.
3. 'Jelly Tiles' can be applied to any smooth clean surface.
4. Tiles are pliable.
5. Wave-pattern 'Jelly Tile'.

2

3

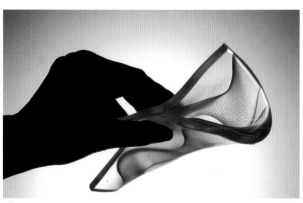

4

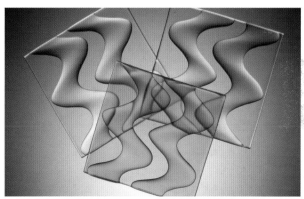

5

1

photoluminescent glass tiles

Tiles that glow in the dark are just one application of photoluminescent pigments developed by the watch industry. These 'afterglow' pigments, generally applied to watch faces so that they can be read in the dark, are nontoxic and nonradioactive. Other common uses are for signage, labelling and in automotive design. Combined with glass tiles, they make a product that is intriguingly decorative.

The tiles are printed on the back with three layers of glass enamel, burnt onto the surface at high temperature. The photoluminescent pigment is contained within one of the enamel layers and combined with two other background colours, red and turquoise.

Characteristics
• Glass tiles that glow in the dark. The photoluminescent pigment, which is the reactive element of the material, requires no power. Instead, it collects UV rays from either natural or artificial light and emits a bright greenish glow for about an hour in the dark.
• The pattern is two-dimensional under lit conditions, three-dimensional in the dark.
• Increases safety by making glass more visible and could potentially help in orientation.
• Nontoxic and nonradioactive.
• Water-resistant.
• Can be used either internally or externally.

Applications
• Currently at prototype stage. Potential uses include any interior application where a tiled surface is desirable, including kitchens and bathrooms, as well as external glazing, partitions and doors.

1.–2. Photoluminescent glass tiles.
3.–4. Table decorated with photoluminescent pattern.

2

3

4

1

LED tiles

LED is undoubtedly the future of lighting. These tiny light-emitting diodes have been around for quite a while in information and display lighting, in standby buttons, oven clocks, car dashboards and countless other everyday applications. In the wake of recent improvements, which mean that they are now cheaper, brighter and available in a wider colour range than before, they are playing a greater role in decorative and practical interior lighting. One such development is the LED tile.

Light that can be built into the fabric of your home opens up exciting decorative possibilities – lit pathways to guide you from place to place, skirting lighting to accentuate architectural form, or evocative controllable displays that change colour or create intriguing patterns.

Types of LED tile

• There are several types of LED tile on the market. The simplest consists of single-colour LED modules inset into ceramic tiles.
• More sophisticated are controllable LED modules that can be programmed to switch between two colours and different rates.
• Most advanced of all are tiles that consist of 144 individual nodes mounted behind a sheet of translucent plastic, each node powered by a microchip that provides a high degree of precision control, enabling images to be created.

Characteristics

• LEDs give off very little heat and last between 80,000 and 100,000 hours (11 years).
• They consume a fraction of the energy of an incandescent bulb – 3 watts.
• New-generation LEDs are much brighter.
• LED tiles require specialist installation. A connecting cable is run from the mains adaptor (and programmer in more sophisticated formats) to the first lit tile. Then each LED tile is connected to the next with a cable that runs up the back of the tiles in the adhesive bed, feeding through the central cutout in the tile to connect, via a mini-plug, with the lighting module. The tiles are bedded as usual with adhesive and grouted.

Applications

• As decorative or accent lighting in many areas of the home.
• As information lighting in bathrooms, stairs, hallways and other places where low-level lighting is an asset for safety.
• To make colourful sophisticated lighting displays.
• Can be used in floors, walls and ceilings.

Finish

• The lighting module must be protected during installation to prevent it from becoming damaged or dirty.

1. LED tiles arranged to create a continuous lit border.
2. Individual LED tiles make a pathway of light.
3. Specialist installation is essential for LED tiles.

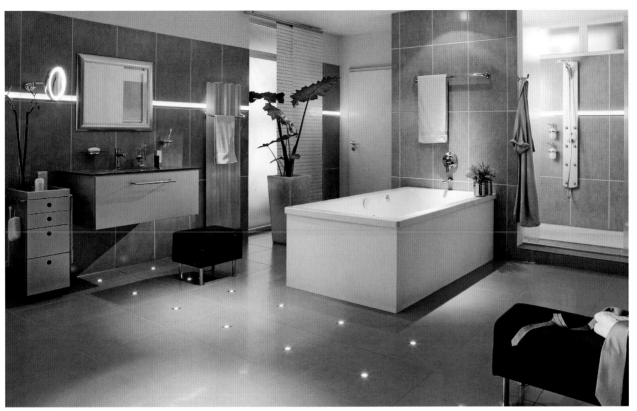

2

3

Above: Luminous LED glass borders in combination with mosaic tiling.

Above: LEDs are incredibly long-lasting and consume very little energy.

textiles & papers

Textiles and decorative papers, traditional elements of the interior decorator's stock in trade, have recently undergone something of a transformation as materials technology has ushered in whole new ways of working. One such advance is in the general area of rapid manufacturing. This comprises a number of techniques that were first developed in order to facilitate the production of prototypes, but which are now being applied to products and materials intended for end use. Another more familiar process is digital printing, which has obvious applications in the creation of patterns and imagery.

But textiles and papers can be 'smart' in other ways, aside from their means of manufacture. Fabric woven with fibre optics, or that shifts its colour and pattern in response to varying electrical charges, interacts with its environment in a subtle and surprising fashion.

Much of the work produced in this area, using new technology, new materials or both, is created by artists and designers, applying cutting-edge engineering in playfully creative ways. From fabric that isn't cut or sewn, to wallpaper patterns you create yourself – the material world is changing out of all recognition.

Characteristics
• Either interactive in some way – using light sources or simply movable stickers – or produced in a technologically sophisticated fashion.
• The use of lasers for cutting or in laser-sintering processes results in textiles and papers that are precision cut or modelled three-dimensionally.
• Many of these products have been created by artist-designers as one-off installations.

Opposite: Electroluminescent fabric: 'Digital Dawn' blind and 'Light Sleeper' bedding.

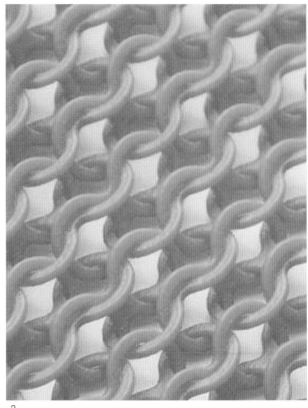

1

2

laser-sintered textiles

Selective laser sintering (SLS) is one of a number of techniques of rapid manufacturing that were first developed as a means of speeding up and simplifying the process of making prototypes. A three-dimensional design is created on the computer. Then a very high-powered laser selectively fuses small particles of powdered material into that 3-D design, by repeatedly scanning cross-sections of the design generated by the computer file onto the surface of the powdered material. After each scan, a fresh layer of powdered material is added until the process is complete.

A number of different powdered materials can be used in this process, including metals such as steel and various types of plastic, including resin, polystyrene and nylon. One application is in the production of architectural models, with information taken directly from CAD files.

Innovative design company Freedom of Creation, founded by Finnish designer Janne Kyttänen, has experimented with laser sintering and produced a number of award-winning products. The MGX lamp series, produced in collaboration with Materialise, feature shades created by 3-D printing, memorably the Lotus lamp, with its polyamide shade formed into the shape of a lotus flower. The same company also produce laser-sintered textiles.

Characteristics
• 3-D woven textile form created without stitching, cutting, knitting or weaving.
• Computer-generation means that custom designs are possible, with variations of size, colour and geometry.
• Unlike other rapid manufacturing techniques, such as stereolithography, supports are not required during the manufacturing process.
• Generates much less waste than standard manufacturing processes.
• Synthetic material.

Applications
• Potentially as wide as for any form of textile.

Finish
• No subsequent finishing is required.
• Care as for synthetic material.

1.–6. Various types of laser-sintered textiles, produced without weaving or sewing.

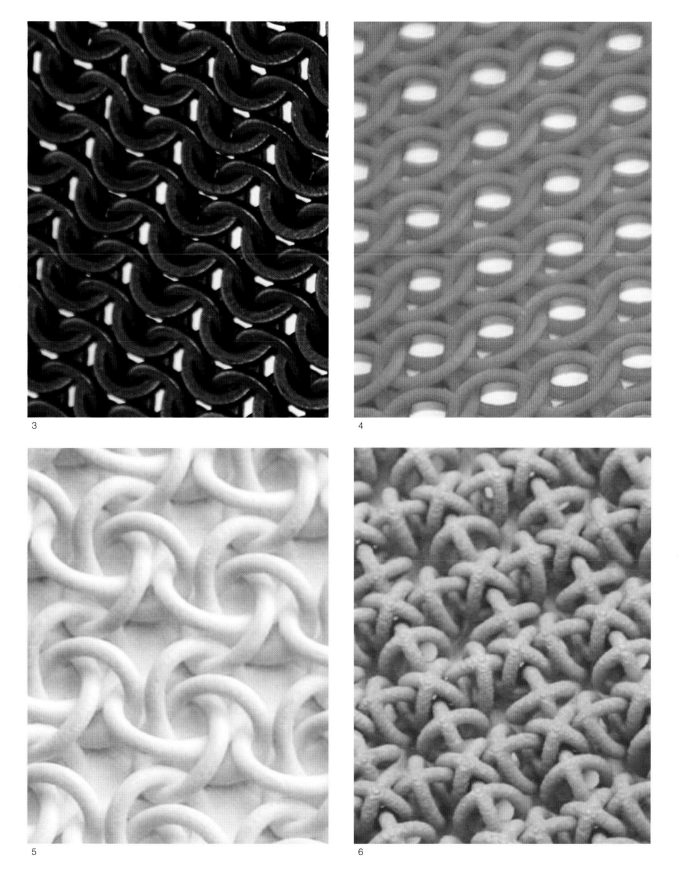

3

4

5

6

laser-cut textiles

A much simpler application of laser technology in textile production is laser cutting. Here, the textile is not built up of layers of powdered material, but simply cut by the laser to create patterns and surface texture. A wide range of materials can be cut in this way, including natural weaves and felted cloths. The effects range from fine filigrees of lace to gentle contours.

1. Laser-cut patterns are very precise.
2. Laser-cut felt.
3. Detail of motif.

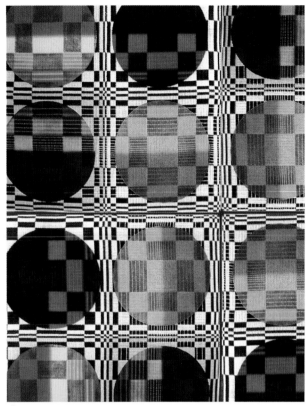

programmable electric textiles

Fabric that changes colour at the flick of a switch is no longer the stuff of science fiction. An American design company called IFM (International Fashion Machines) has patented the technological process that allows it to produce fabrics such as 'Electric Plaid'™, an electronically controllable colour-change textile. The fabric can be programmed to display changing patterns across the surface or to make colour move like a wave from one end to the other. Other smart textiles produced by the same company include 'fuzzy' dimmers and light controls. Such e-textiles are very tactile, expressive and dynamic, adding the dimensions of time and motion to what would otherwise be an entirely static material.

The textile is produced in individual hand-woven modules that incorporate four to eight strands of electronic yarns (depending on the size) and hand-printed in two to three layers of colour-changing inks. When activated, the conductive yarns produce the colour-changing patterns. Modules can be grouped, rotated and arranged to form panels of different sizes and rectilinear shapes.

Characteristics
• Programmable colour-changing fabric.
• Larger panels can be created by networking modules or alternating inactive modules with active ones for greater coverage.
• Includes drive electronics that can be integrated into the piece at the back or located out of the way.
• Comes with a power supply that must be plugged into an electrical outlet controlled by a switch: one power supply per eight modules. One dedicated circuit supports 16 modules.
• Comes in many standard patterns; custom designs and colours are also possible, including text and imagery.
• Can be programmed to run automatically or can be interactive, triggered by different types of sensors.
• Sensitive to UV light. Eventually, the colour-changing pattern becomes inactive.

Applications
• Can be hung on the wall like paintings, panels or fabric hangings.
• Can be bent or curved, but in one direction only – either horizontally or vertically.

Finish
• No further finishing required.
• Keep out of direct sunlight.

1. 'Electric Plaid' is an electronically controlled colour-change textile.
2. Detail of 'Electric Plaid'.

1

2

3

electroluminescent fabric

British artist/designer Rachel Wingfield looks to the natural world as a source of inspiration for her interactive fabrics. Using electroluminescent technology, fabric can be made responsive to its environment, reacting to changes in light levels by emitting pulses of light or 'growing' a pattern across the surface of the textile.

Two relatively recent projects that demonstrate the potential of this technique are 'Digital Dawn Blind' and 'Light Sleeper' bed linen. In the case of the blind, images of foliage are printed onto the textile with phosphorescent inks. Light sensors detect changing levels of light so that the foliage appears to grow or die back as the light changes. The natural energy of the sun is stored during the day and used later to illuminate the blind, emulating the process of photosynthesis. The bed linen was conceived as a way of aiding sufferers of SAD (seasonal affective disorder) by mimicking the effect of early morning light. The gentlest of wake-up calls, the bed linen simulates a natural dawn by gradually beginning to glow in a pulsing, breathing rhythm over a 15–20 minute period.

Characteristics

• Fabric printed with phosphorescent inks to react to changing light levels.
• Specialist commission.

Application

Potentially wide application in furnishings.

1.–2. 'Digital Dawn' blind made using electroluminescent technology.
3. Cushion cover.
4. 'Light Sleeper' bedding.

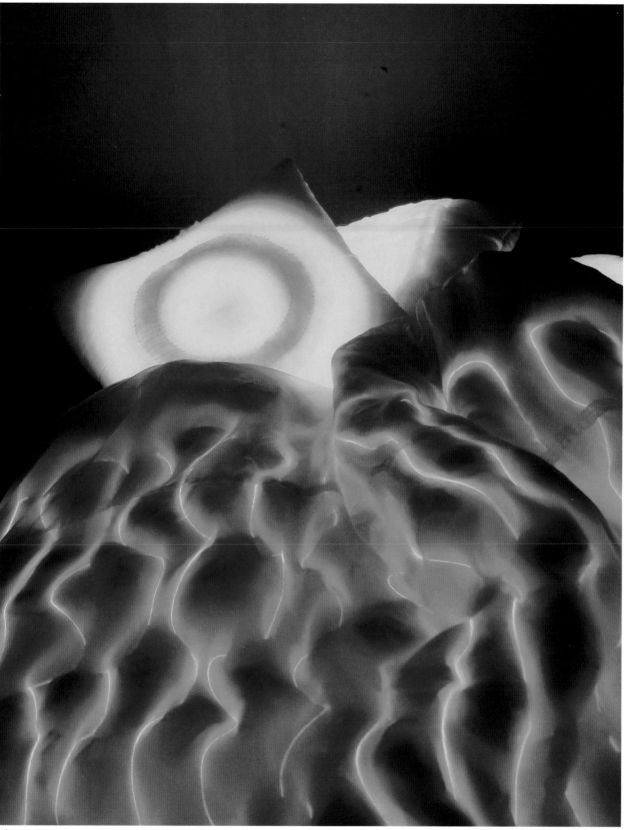

4

1

2

textiles woven with optical fibres

Fibre optics is a relatively established form of lighting that is increasingly finding its way into domestic applications. Light is directed at the ends of fine coated strands of acrylic or fibreglass and travels down the length of these strands to emerge at the end as many individual small starry points. Because the light source – a light box – can be remotely located from the area where the light is finally emitted, this type of lighting is ideal for underwater or wet areas, or any application where delicate items might be damaged by heat or UV radiation – museums, for example.

Recently, designers have been using fibre optics in combination with other fibres to create intriguing illuminated weaves. Bending or sandblasting fibre optics allows light to be emitted from the side as well as the ends, a feature that British designer Sharon Marston has explored in her chandeliers.

One of the most exciting new developments, however, is the use of optical fibres to create illuminated textiles. The product of much research and experimentation, the light-emitting fibres are the type used in subnuclear physics experiments. Woven with conventional fibres, the result is a fine transparent starry mesh that can be lit in different colours. The textile, marketed under brand name Luminex®, has potentially wide applications in clothing, soft furnishing and signage.

Characteristics

• Light-emitting nonreflective textile. Can be illuminated in different colours.

• Fine transparent mesh that shines like a starry sky when lit up.

• May be powered by a transformer, such as a mobile-phone battery charger, or directly by battery.

Applications

• Curtains, tablecloths, seat covers and similar soft-furnishing applications.

Finish

• The fabric should be treated as delicate.

1. 'April' chandelier by Sharon Marston.
2. 'Autumn' chandelier by Sharon Marston.
3. 'Miami' panel by Sharon Marston.
4. 'Pleat' by Sharon Marston.
5. 'Luminex' textile incorporating optical fibres.

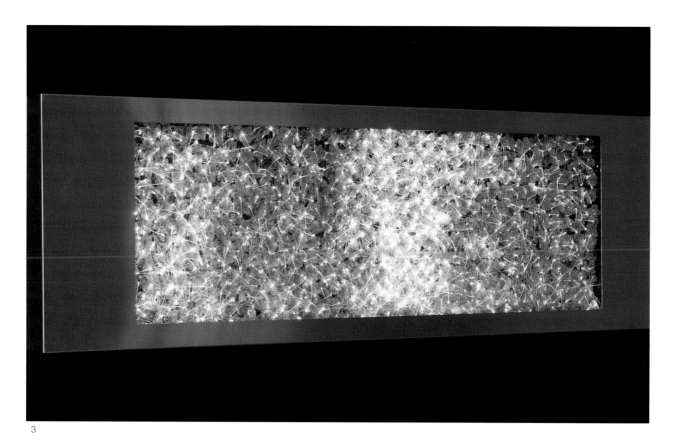

3

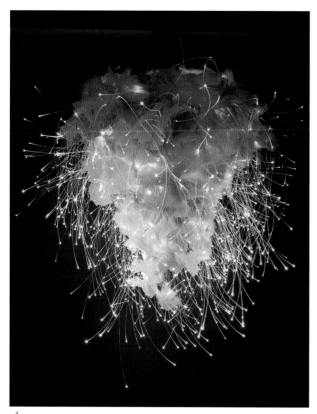

4

5

1

2

interactive wallpaper

Responsive walls are dynamic and poetic. On the simplest, 'low-tech' level, interactivity can be achieved by involving the user in the creative process. This is the intention of British designer Rachel Kelly, whose interactive papers are designed to be customized with lace-cut vinyl stickers – the consumer can enhance the basic pattern through their application.

At the high-tech end of the spectrum are smart papers that respond to their surroundings. One Swedish design studio devised a project in which a pattern appeared gradually on paper after exposure to UV light – the paper was patterned with photochromic inks.

'Blumen', a project by Rachel Wingfield and Mattias Gmachi,

uses electroluminescent technology to create kinetic room dividers. Strictly speaking textiles, the panels are, however, intended to be displayed flat as 'wallpaper'. The pattern is a repeating leaf motif, which luminesces thanks to the application of electroluminescent ink applied to the textile using a special ink-jet printer. A thin electric wire delivers current to each patterned area and allows parts of the design to be controlled individually. The use of different sensors allows the pattern to develop in response to different environmental factors.

1. 'Blumen' electro-luminescent wall panel by Rachel Wingfield and Mattias Gmachi.
2. & 4. 'Corso' photoluminescent paper in daylight and in the dark.

3

4

5

6

7

3., 6. & 7. Interactive wallpaper by Rachel Kelly can
be customized by laser-cut adhesive stickers (5.).

1

2

3

4   1.–4. 'Blumen' by Rachel Wingfield and Mattias Gmachi features a repeating leaf motif that luminesces. Different parts of the 'wallpaper' can be controlled individually.

interactive flooring

On the very simplest level, any surface we touch we interact with, and floors are no exception. When we move from place to place, the materials that we encounter underfoot reveal a wide range of qualities through the way they feel and sound – texture, resilience, degree of smoothness, degree of hardness and so on. New developments in interactive flooring amplify this experience by making it more visible or audible – floors that light up as you walk on them, tracing your footsteps; floors that make noises in response to pressure; floors that change colour.

An interactive floor that creates shifting patterns of light and colour is a great way of enhancing a club atmosphere and some of the projects that have been developed in this field have been carried out with such applications in mind. But touch-sensitive flooring could also play a role in security, serving as an alarm that senses and detects intruders. There is also the possibility that lit pathways could be used to orient people in a pre-arranged way through a space, following a trail of LEDs. One designer has constructed individual light-up floor tiles that show one of three primary shades according to how much pressure is exerted upon them, envisaging the product as a way of engaging small children creatively in their surroundings. Whatever the form, these playful skins bring a new dimension to material quality.

Most of these designs are at prototype stage only, or have been explored in one-off installations; some interactive flooring systems, including one that consists of small networked tiles that light up when they are stepped on, are available to rent for special occasions such as exhibitions or events.

Opposite: 'Light Fader', an interactive light floor by Rogier Sterk.

Smart carpet
Characteristics
• Smart carpet comprises a weave of conductive fibre studded with sensor chips and LEDs. Hooked up to a power source and computer, the carpet becomes 'aware'. Potential uses include guided pathways and fire and security alarms.

Sensitive carpet
Characteristics
• Sensitive carpet, capable of detecting footsteps, relies on conductive powder embedded in a multilayered fabric. When the fabric is compressed, its electrical properties change.
• Available in tiles from 10 x 10cm to 100 x 100cm.
• Can be cut and joined.
• Different levels of detectable pressure can be set.

Interactive light flooring
Characteristics
• Developed as a prototype by Rogier Sterk, interactive light flooring leaves a trail of prints of light wherever the surface is touched. The trail remains behind for about a minute. The same modular system can be used without light when applied over a transparent intermediate floor, in which case the footprints are visible as transparent shapes in an otherwise uniformly coloured background.
• The basic construction of the modules incorporates a top layer of tough, scratch-resistant plastic and a bottom layer of thick flooring glass. In between is a thin film of coloured fluid. Each module rests on a support structure that houses a light installation. The pressure of footprints on the floor displaces the fluid temporarily and allows the light to shine through.

sustainable

sustainable introduction

Homes devour great quantities of materials, both in construction and in surfaces and finishes. Choosing materials with sound eco credentials helps to minimize the harm done to our planet. The materials covered in this section generally represent good green alternatives – simple substitutions for more familiar and, ecologically speaking, more contentious versions. But that is not to say that all those detailed elsewhere in this book are necessarily ruled out for the green-minded consumer.

When it comes to choosing materials responsibly, sustainability is a key concept. It means selecting materials that do not deplete natural resources, do not damage ecosystems and do not pose a problem for future generations. Another factor that comes into the equation is embodied energy. Our homes use energy directly for heating, cooling and power. But materials represent energy in an embodied form – the energy that was required to extract them, transport them, process them, deliver them and work with them. The less a material has to be worked before it is used, and the shorter distance it has to travel, the lower its embodied energy. Materials that do not contain toxic elements, or that can be maintained without recourse to synthetic products and preparations, are also preferable.

Increasingly, however, eco design has embraced a more pluralistic approach. For example, using small quantities of a material, such as steel, that is high in embodied energy can be a good strategy if this makes a building last longer or improves its structural performance. Materials with high thermal mass, such as concrete and stone, can play an important role in passive heating strategies. Materials that are composed of recycled synthetics and that are themselves recyclable represent a good way of addressing the plastics problem. And while many eco alternatives direct us back to a low-tech approach, technology also has a role to play – low-E glazing, for example, has an insulating coating that keeps heat indoors and permits the construction of large openings that wash interiors with light and so reduce dependence on artificial sources.

Above: Sisal natural-fibre flooring is made of renewable materials.

alternatives to wood

Properly sourced from approved sustainably managed plantations, and in solid rather than composite form, wood is a good green material. It doesn't require much in the way of processing and it derives from a living renewable source. Furthermore, it lends itself to both salvage and recycling. Properly maintained, a solid wood surface, or a wood with a thick veneer that can be resanded, will last for years.

Composite wood products, such as MDF and particleboard, represent an efficient use of timber because they make use of sawdust, chippings and whatever else is left over after sawing and dimensioning solid timber (up to two-thirds of the tree in some cases) that would otherwise go to waste. However, such products are often bonded with chemicals that have been shown to have a deleterious effect on human health and adverse environmental consequences. One exception is plywood; although it does contain formaldehyde, the chemical is present at much lower, safer concentrations.

Reasons to consider wood alternatives

• Demand for construction timber far outstrips supply. While international bodies are getting better at monitoring forestry projects and tracking the vicissitudes of the timber trade, in many circumstances it is difficult to be absolutely sure that a particular batch of wood has come from an approved source.

• Softwoods, which are the mainstay of the building industry, require protection from fire, moisture and pests, which is generally delivered in the form of chemical treatment. Eco finishing treatments include borax, which is used as a wood preservative, natural waxes, oils and stains.

• In construction, new manufactured wood products, such as parallam and glulam – plies of wood glued and laminated under high pressure to produce structural members capable of spanning great distances – are increasingly a preferred eco option. But when it comes to surfaces and finishes, there are a number of alternatives that look and perform just as well as wood.

Opposite: Palmwood flooring and palmwood plywood are every bit as attractive as hardwood.

1

2

bamboo

Ecologically speaking, bamboo is something of a wonder plant. A woody grass rather than a true tree, it is incredibly fast-growing and fast-spreading, achieving a height of 1.5m within months and full maturity at five to six years. Its cultivation requires little human intervention and it does not require fertilization or the application of pesticides. Bamboo improves poor soil, cuts down carbon dioxide emissions and is fully renewable.

There are 1,500 species of bamboo, but most of the bamboo used in the production of bamboo products comes from China and Indonesia. The associated transport costs mean that in this sense bamboo is high in terms of embodied energy, but its other credentials weigh heavily in the balance.

Strands or strips of bamboo fibre can be laminated into boards, planks, panels and veneers. Other uses include textiles (see page 230) and papers (see page 238). The best bamboo comes from manufacturers who control the process from harvest to end product and who are able to guarantee that only a small proportion of formaldehyde is used in the laminating process. Harvested too early, bamboo can be as soft as fir. Mature bamboo, however, is harder than maple and oak.

Characteristics

• Renewable, plentiful resource that is fast-growing.

• Strips or strands are laminated into a variety of products, including flooring-grade boards and planks, panels and veneers.

• Different degrees of hardness are available, with the toughest surpassing maple and oak in strength and durability.

• Boards and panels are available in different dimensions and with matching finishing details, such as mouldings and trim.

• Very stable.

• Available in vertical grain, flat grain and a mixture of the two, which increases strength, hardness and stability.

• A variety of woody colours from pale to darker shades. Some types of bamboo flooring feature natural colour variation that makes for a lively surface.

Applications

• Flooring. Condition flooring by storing it in the area where it will be used for 72 hours. Install by nailing or stapling, or by gluing with a water-based adhesive. The subfloor may be plywood, concrete or timber.

• Panelling and cladding.

• Counters and worktops.

Finish

• Many bamboo products come ready-finished.

• Care as for hardwood (see page 40).

1. Bamboo flooring is incredibly hardwearing.
2. Flat-grain bamboo flooring.
3.–4. Bamboo canes used as wall cladding.
5. Bamboo flooring can be nailed or glued in place.

3

4

5

1

palm

Coconut palms are grown in abundance in plantations around the world, specifically for their nuts. As a palm ages, it increases in height until after about 80–100 years it is no longer able to produce nuts because nutrients have too far to travel from the ground to the top. Once a palm becomes nonproducing, it is cut and replaced with a shorter, younger palm.

Palmwood is derived from those cut palms that would otherwise go to waste. Unlike wood, the palm fibre is darker and harder at the perimeter; the central portions are soft and light. Palmwood is manufactured by cutting, slicing and kiln-drying the raw material before laminating the strands and bonding them with a nontoxic adhesive.

Characteristics
• Abundant, renewable natural source.
• Multiple laminated layers produce a stable and durable wood-like material.
• Available in tongue-and-groove planks cut to various lengths and as panels and plywood.
• Characteristic dark colour with different graining patterns.

Applications
• Flooring. Store flooring in the area where it will be used for 72 hours before installation. Nail or glue in place over a dry, level subfloor (plywood, concrete or timber flooring).
• Not suitable for very wet areas.
• Panelling and cladding.

Finish
• Supplied unfinished or pre-finished.
• Care as for hardwood (see page 40).

1. Palmwood flooring in a bedroom.
2. Palmwood has a characteristic dark colour.
3. Palmwood ply.
4. Unfinished palmwood flooring.
5. Stained palmwood flooring.

2

3

4

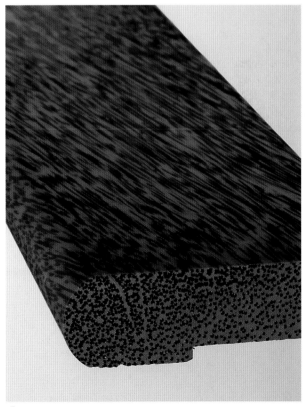

5

1

cork

Cork in various formats has been around for years as an unpretentious, if not utilitarian, floor and wall covering. It comes from a harvestable, renewable resource: the bark of the evergreen cork oak (*Quercus suber*), a tree native to the Mediterranean region. Portugal is the largest producer of cork today.

Cork trees shed their bark naturally every nine or ten years and can carry on producing cork for 200 years or more, which means that cork can be harvested without damage to the tree. The cork used to make tiles, sheets and other formats for interior surfaces is actually the waste product of the cork harvested to make bottle stoppers – which makes it a recycled material as well as a harvestable one.

Cork has a cellular structure and is composed of 90 per cent air-like gas, sealed within each microscopic cell by a waxy substance called suberin. As a result, the material is very light and cushioned, and springs back into shape after it has been depressed. Suberin also contributes to the material's natural fire-resistance.

Previously, cork granules were bound together with adhesives containing formaldehyde, which compromised its eco credentials. Now, though, many companies are producing cork using environmentally friendly water-based pigments, solvents and adhesives.

Characteristics

• Derives from a harvestable, renewable source. Recycled product of the cork bottle-stopper industry.
• Warm and resilient underfoot. Comfortable to walk on.
• Excellent thermal- and sound-insulating qualities.
• Antibacterial, hypoallergenic, resists rot, mould and fire.
• Produced in tiles and sheets of various dimensions and thicknesses. Cork-faced floating is also available that snaps and locks into place.
• Some cork tiles have bevelled edges, which allow for expansion and contraction.
• Mostly found in woody shades, but can be brightly coloured.
• Easy to work with. Damaged tiles can be lifted and replaced.

Applications

• Flooring, especially in areas where extra comfort is required underfoot. Not suitable for areas of heavy traffic. Generally applied with adhesive.
• Wall cladding.

Finish

• Some types of cork tile come ready-finished. Otherwise, sealing is necessary.
• Wax is an eco alternative to polyurethane seals.

1. Cork-clad ceilings and walls add textural depth to a clean-lined contemporary home.
2. Cork is warm and inherently soundproofing.
3. Cork is an inexpensive covering derived from renewable sources.
4. Cork-clad wall on a staircase.

2

3

4

recycled wood

Wood lends itself naturally to being recycled, reused and salvaged – which means that there is no excuse for the fact that wood, together with plastic, makes up the greatest proportion of what is dumped in landfill sites. In years gone by, many building materials were reused time and again and it was not uncommon, for example, for ships' timbers to find their way into domestic homes as beams and mantelpieces.

In many instances, recycling can begin at home. You can renovate old floorboards, rather than installing a new floor covering. Similarly, you can upgrade fitted kitchens and other types of storage by retaining the carcases and simply replacing the doors and drawer fronts. If you are bringing reclaimed wood into your home, make sure that it does not harbour woodworm or any other infestation.

Types of reclaimed wood

• Salvaged wooden features and fittings, such as doors, panelling and fireplaces. Good sources are architectural salvage yards, antiques markets and similar outlets. If made of softwood, such features are often available stripped of old finishes. Hardwood features and fittings tend to be rarer and more expensive as a result.

• Reclaimed floorboards and other types of wood flooring. Old boards can be denailed and remilled to even out dimensions and provide a smoother surface. Antique parquet, particularly if the provenance is known, is highly sought-after because of its unique patina and is correspondingly costly.

• Railway sleepers can be used in the garden to make pathways or terraces and to enclose areas of raised planting.

Opposite: Reclaimed boards used as wall panelling.

1

recycled decking

The vogue for outdoor decking has put even greater pressure on the world's stock of hardwoods and softwoods, particularly teak, ipe and Western red cedar. Even where softwood decking is installed, it requires intensive maintenance in the form of chemical treatment to extend its life and provide moisture-resistance. An eco-friendly alternative is a wood polymer composite made out of post-production softwood waste and post-consumer polyethylene waste and that is itself 100 per cent recyclable.

Characteristics
• A composite product that is totally recyclable.
• Available as decking, posts, rails, fencing panels and in other formats for external use.
• Comes in wood shades or strong colours.
• Reasonably convincing as a wood lookalike.
• Slip-resistant, splinter-free and rotproof.

Applications
• Decking.
• Other garden uses include fencing, trellises, edging and pergola beams.

Finish
• No maintenance is required, except for light sweeping

1. Recycled timber makes an attractive garden feature.
2. Railway sleepers used to make garden decking.
3. Retaining wall built out of railway sleepers.

2

3

eco glass

In all but the hottest climates glass is indispensable in building, allowing light into the interior while keeping the weather out. This is not simply a matter of preference and psychological wellbeing, but is backed up by legislation. In the UK, for example, all 'habitable' rooms must have at least one window. Until a few decades ago, most homes featured windows of only a relatively restricted size. In contemporary design, however, the trend is for using greater expanses of glass, which unfortunately has the potential to compromise a building's energy efficiency seriously, with vast amounts of heat drained from the interior after dark, and temperatures raised uncomfortably in warm weather. Recently, new types of glass, such as low-E glass, have been developed to address this problem. Installing highly insulated units in double- or triple-glazed versions is also a good energy-saving strategy.

Glass is made out of basic ingredients – soda, sand and lime – which are abundant and widely available. However, its production, which entails melting those ingredients at vast temperatures, is very costly in terms of energy. One saving grace is that glass is readily recyclable with no loss of purity or clarity, and schemes for sorting and collecting glass are well established in many areas. Although such recycling schemes generally provide material that is turned back into bottles and jars, recycled float glass for external façades and other uses is also available, along with recycled glass tiles that can be used as a substitute for ceramic tiles and cast glass tiles.

Characteristics
- Energy-saving glass comes in a variety of formats, the most popular being low-E (low-emissivity) glass that is coated with a microscopic layer that reflects heat back into the interior.
- Virtually indistinguishable from clear glass.
- Enhanced energy-saving can be achieved by incorporating low-E glass in double- or triple-glazed units.
- Framing and construction of glazed openings has a direct bearing on energy performance.

Opposite: Low-E glass helps to save energy in areas where there are expanses of glazing.

1

2

low-emissivity glass

Ordinary glass absorbs and radiates heat on the colder surface. In cold weather this surface is the external face of the glass or the outer pane in the case of a double-glazed unit. To prevent heat from being lost in this way, low-E glass is coated with a microscopic layer of metallic oxide that reflects heat back into the interior. The basic principle is the same as that low-tech strategy of placing sheets of foil behind radiators to reflect heat back into the room.

Low-E glass is designed to be used in double- or triple-glazed units, not as single glazing. It is installed as the inner pane, with the coating facing into the gap between the glass layers. Different types of coatings are available to provide high solar gain, moderate solar gain or low solar gain, with the high-solar-gain glass being suitable for climates where most energy is consumed in heating and low-solar-gain glass for climates where most energy is consumed in cooling. Another important factor is siting. In a cold or temperate climate, for example, using low-E glass in double-glazed south-facing units reduces the U-value virtually to nil, with the amount of heat lost being balanced by the amount of heat gain from the sun.

Characteristics

• Coated glass with a low U-value. A double-glazed unit that incorporates low-E glass has a similar U-value to a triple-glazed unit.

• Virtually the same in appearance as clear float glass.

• Available in a range of dimensions.

Applications

• Any glazing application where there is the potential for unwelcome heat loss or gain.

• Conservatories, glazed extensions and toplighting.

Finish

• Maintain as for standard glass.

• Because low-E glazing looks almost indistinguishable from standard glass, care must be taken during installation to confirm its presence by checking with a coating detector.

1. Low-E glass minimizes heat loss in glazed rooms.
2. Low-E glass has virtually the same appearance as standard glass.
3. Low-E glass is particularly useful for top glazing.

3

1

2

highly insulated glazed units

Installing double glazing in place of old single-glazed windows is a popular form of home improvement. For most consumers, saving money on energy bills is often more persuasive than environmental issues, along with the fact that uPVC-framed double glazing is virtually maintenance-free.

Double- or triple-glazed units trap air between the panes, which insulates against heat loss and helps to reduce noise transmission. Installing low-E glass as the inner pane in a unit reduces the U-values still further. In very high-specification windows, the cavities are filled with argon or krypton gas, which conduct less heat than air.

Window construction and frames also have a bearing on the thermal performance. One of the most popular materials used to make double-glazing units is uPVC. It's cheap, has good insulating properties, can be fashioned into a range of profiles and designs and requires little maintenance. However, as one of the most problematic of plastics, it cannot be recommended on ecological grounds. The best insulating material for window frames is wood, either softwood, which is not very durable and needs frequent refinishing, or naturally weather-resistant hardwood, whose sustainable sourcing may cause a problem. Metal frames – such as aluminium – are very long-lasting but have high embodied energy and

compromise the window's insulating properties dramatically. Composite frames – such as those made of wood powder-coated with aluminium – can offer the best of both worlds.

Replacing original windows with double-glazing does not win universal approval in architectural circles because of its visual effect on the elevational detailing of period houses. In conservation areas, or if your home is listed, you may be prohibited from making this type of alteration.

Characteristics
• A range of highly insulating units, double- or triple-glazed.
• May include low-E glass.
• Cavities may be filled with argon or krypton gas.

• Available off-the-shelf in standard sizes and shapes; bespoke designs are possible.
• Very high-specification windows include integral blinds operated by controls on the outside.
• Price depends on specification and framing material.

Applications
• Substitute glazing to prevent heat loss and reduce draughts.

Finish
• Subsequent maintenance depends on the framing material.

1. Double- or tripled-glazed units are very energy-efficient.
2. Framing material has an important impact on the U-values of glazing.
3. Bespoke glazed units can be made to high specifications.

3

recycled plastics

Our disposable consumer society generates a vast amount of waste and a significant proportion of that is plastic. Plastic is cheap, which encourages people to discard it more readily, and it is ubiquitous, a significant or sole component of a huge range of products from packaging to CDs. More than 15 million mobile phones are thrown away every year in the UK alone. Reuse is one way to cut down on plastic waste; another is recycling.

'Plastic' is a generic term for a broad family of different polymer types. The highest-quality recycled plastic comes from waste of a single plastic type. Sorting plastics into like with like was once problematic, but it is easier now that labelling is mandatory. Recycled plastic can be made from plastic bottles, crushed CDs, polystyrene cups, mobile-phone casings and even children's wellies.

Aside from its eco credentials, one of the most appealing aspects of recycled plastic is its vivid colours and patterning. The nature of the recycling process, as well as the waste ingredients, throw up random streaks and mottling that inject the material with striking vitality. The material is also through-coloured, which increases its creative applications.

After collection and sorting, the waste plastic is cleaned and shredded into flakes. This raw material is then measured into a mould, placed in a hydraulic press and subjected to heat and immense pressure. The combination of heat and pressure turns the flakes into rigid boards or soft sheets, depending on the source material.

Opposite: Recycled plastic sheets used as wall cladding introduce a vivid accent of colour and pattern.
Overleaf:
1.–2. Recycled plastic sheet made of discarded children's wellies.
3. Recycled plastic sheet made of plastic bottles.
4. Recycled plastic sheet made of plastic pipes.
5. Recycled plastic sheet made of mobile-phone covers.

Characteristics
- Most recycled plastic comes in the form of rigid boards 1200 x 800mm and 6–8mm thick. These can be worked like wood-based boards with saws and drills, and fastened with screws, bolts, clips and similar fixings.
- Plastic recycled from children's wellies is softer and thinner (3mm thick).
- Both types are safe, nontoxic and eco-friendly.
- Do not expose to excessive heat, boiling water or organic solvents.
- Colours may fade in direct sunlight.

Applications
- Rigid sheets or panels: worksurfaces, shelving, cladding, furniture, screens and partitions.
- Soft sheets: table coverings, mats and seat covers.
- Not recommended for ceiling cladding.

Finish
- Boards have either a matt or semi-gloss finish that requires no further finishing. Car polish can be applied to increase the shine.
- Maintain by washing away surface dirt using a mild detergent and warm water. Avoid abrasive cleansers and solvents such as nail-polish remover and paint stripper.
- Any surface scratches can be sanded smooth using sandpaper.

1

2

3

4

5

1

2

Durat®

A solid composite made of 50 per cent recycled plastics and that is itself completely recyclable, Durat® is a sophisticated material that is available in a range of different designs and formats, from worktops with integral sinks to bathtubs. Custom designs are also possible. The manufacturing process allows for seamless panels many metres long. Manufactured by a Finnish company, Durat has a clean-lined and minimalist aesthetic, with colour a particularly strong suit.

Characteristics

• 100 per cent recyclable material made of 50 per cent recycled polyester-based plastics.
• Warm and silky to the touch.
• Through-coloured; the finish gives the impression of depth.
• Wide range of standard colours; edging and patterns can also be specified.
• Available in a design collection of baths, shower trays, worktops, basins, tables, stools and benches; bespoke pieces can be made.
• Very resistant to water, wear and some chemicals.
• Seamless panels can be specified. Alternatively, seams can be sanded to make them almost invisible.
• Can be worked using woodworking tools.

Applications

• As ready-made baths, basins, shower trays, worktops with integral sinks, and furniture.
• As cladding, particularly in wet areas.

Finish

• This material requires no subsequent finishing.
• Easy to clean.
• Scratches can be sanded smooth with sandpaper.

1. Black bathtub made of Durat.
2. Durat handbasin. The material feels warm to the touch.
3. Durat is easy to clean and any scratches can be sanded smooth.
4. Square basin.
5. Seamless bathtub.

3

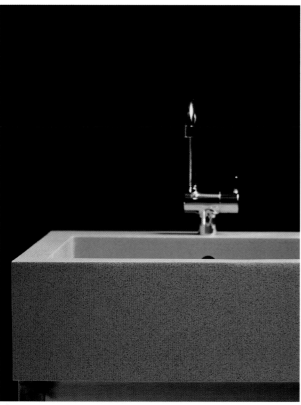

4

5

textiles & papers

For the ecologically minded, natural textiles and papers, which come from readily available, renewable, biodegradable and recyclable sources, and which are not processed using huge amounts of energy like synthetic materials, are obviously preferable. However, while it is usually relatively straightforward to confirm that a paper or textile is wholly natural in composition, it is not always easy to determine whether it has been chemically treated in some way that is harmful to health, the environment or both.

Cotton is a case in point. Because the cotton plant is so vulnerable to a wide range of pests, chemicals are routinely used by growers to protect their crops. Chemical bleaches are applied to most cotton; coloured cotton is chemically dyed and fixed. And, like many other natural materials used in clothing and upholstery, cotton may subsequently be treated to promote fire-retardance, or to make it easy-care and noncreasing.

Using natural textiles and papers

• Always choose the right weight of material for the job it has to do, to prevent wastage during installation and more frequent replacement necessitated by excessive wear. Furnishing-weight fabric should be used for upholstery rather than the lighter fabric used for clothing. You can paper walls with almost any type of paper, but the more robust weights will last longer and be easier to paste up without tearing.

• Check labels carefully. Qualities such as 'crease-resistance' and 'easy-care' tend to indicate that chemicals have been applied during finishing. Formaldehyde is the treatment used to make fabric and other textiles more fire-retardant (which is a legal requirement in some parts of the world). Similarly, papers can be treated with a thin layer of vinyl to make them water-resistant.

• Many natural materials are compromised by synthetic backings or underlayers. Try to source natural or recyclable underlays if possible.

• Another way natural materials can be compromised is through the use of synthetic adhesives. Water-soluble, solvent-free adhesives are available as an alternative.

Opposite: Coir matting banded with leather strips.

natural fibres

The extended family of natural fibres includes firm favourites such as cotton, linen and wool, as well as more exotic types such as sisal, jute, coir and seagrass. All come from abundant renewable resources and are processed with little energy. As mentioned previously, surface chemical treatment, synthetic underlays and adhesives, and chemicals used during the growing cycle can compromise eco-worthiness.

Many of these fibres are available woven into floor coverings or textiles for soft furnishings and paper-backed for use as wallpaper. Some take dyes better than others; soft, organic natural colourways are the norm.

Types of natural fibre

• **Bamboo** (See also pages 206–7 and 238.) As well as being made into boards, planks and panels, bamboo fibres can be woven into mats and rugs and even into textiles. Bamboo fabric is incredibly soft because of the roundness of the fibres and is available made up into clothing such as T-shirts.

• **Coir** The fibre derives from the hairy husk of the coconut and is woven into strong, resilient floor coverings (carpets, rugs or doormats). Coir is exceptionally hardwearing, but it is prickly underfoot and does not dye easily.

• **Cotton** Woven into textiles and widely used in clothing and bed linen, cotton breathes and absorbs moisture, which makes it feel good next to the skin. Unbleached and organic cotton is preferable; vegetable dyes can also be used to colour the fabric.

• **Felt** Felt is matted wool. The textile can be used to make clothing, hangings, tablemats, runners and a host of other soft-furnishing applications. Felt is a natural shock-absorber and insulator.

• **Hemp** The potential of hemp has been overlooked somewhat because of its narcotic effects when smoked. Nevertheless, the plant has thousands of other uses, some of which have been around for many, many centuries. Hemp is a very strong fibre and naturally resistant to rot and salt water; it does not fade in strong light. The hemp that is grown to make textiles has no active narcotic ingredients, is highly productive and requires no chemical support during the growing cycle. Hemp can be woven into ropes and coarse canvas; when blended with other, softer natural fibres, the fabric is lighter and more comfortable and has many potential applications.

• **Jute** In long use for making ropes and hessian cloth, and as a natural backing for carpet and linoleum, jute fibres derive from a subtropical plant native to India. Jute weaves used as floor coverings are softer than sisal or coir and suitable for areas of light traffic only, such as bedrooms, where their texture is also kinder to bare feet.

• **Linen** Like cotton, linen derives from a plant, in this case flax. However, flax does not require such heavy use of pesticides. Very strong, long-lasting, cool and absorbent,

1

which makes it prized for bed linen. It is generally bleached, chemically dyed and treated for flame-retardance; eco alternatives include unbleached linen dyed with vegetable dyes. Linen can also be woven into floor coverings, suitable for light traffic use only.

• **Nettle** Most familiar as the garden weed that stings, nettles have also been used for centuries to make textiles. Because the fibres are hollow, nettle cloth is naturally insulating. Crops require no pesticides or chemical treatment during the growing cycle.

• **Paper** As well as being used as a wall covering, paper can be woven into a surprisingly durable floor covering, generally in the form of mats or area rugs. These textiles have an appealing crispness that

suits contemporary interiors.

• **Rattan** Fibres from southeast Asian grasses and woody plants are woven into products such as baskets, matting and chair seats. Overharvesting, leading to habitat destruction, has been a problem in some areas, so materials should be sourced from sustainably managed plantations.

• **Seagrass** Fibres come from a grass native to China. One of the cheaper natural-fibre weaves, seagrass mats and floor coverings are smooth, hardwearing and naturally water-resistant, which means that they cannot be dyed. Slightly slippery underfoot and not suitable for use on stairs for that reason.

• **Silk** A supremely soft and luxurious material woven from the fibres of silkworm cocoons.

2

1

Most silk is imported, which adds to the embodied energy costs. It is generally treated with mothproofing chemicals and chemically dyed.

• **Sisal** The fibre comes from the agave plant and is very strong and hardwearing. Sisal rugs, mats or carpeting can be used in areas of heavy traffic; weaves are softer than coir but rougher than wool. Sisal is not water-resistant and will stain if wet. This characteristic allows it to be easily dyed and the aesthetic range is greater than for other natural fibres.

• **Wool** When we think of wool, we tend to think of sheep's wool, but the fabric is woven from the fibres of other animals, too, such as goats and alpacas. Warm, absorbent

and naturally more flame-resistant than cotton or linen, wool is generally treated with a moth-repellent; wool carpets and rugs are also usually given a stain-resistant treatment and may have synthetic backing, synthetic underlay or a percentage of synthetic fibres added to give improved wear performance. Natural wool products are untreated and dyed with vegetable dyes.

Characteristics

• Fibres can be woven into a wide range of textile weights.
• Natural-fibre flooring is nonoily and hypoallergenic.
• Made from renewable sources and biodegradable.
• Natural-fibre flooring can be laid wall to wall like carpet or is

available as rugs, runners and mats. Pattern tends to derive from the weave – herringbone and bouclé are two varieties.
• Many natural fibres are not stain-resistant.

Applications

• Textiles of appropriate weight can be used for blinds, window treatments, soft furnishings, bed linen and table linen.
• Floor coverings. Natural-fibre floor coverings should be laid professionally over underlay. Choose natural underlay or underlay made of recycled waste synthetic materials.

Finish

• Surface treatment with chemicals to improve fire-retardance or deter moths

can undermine eco credentials.
• Most natural fibres stain readily; mop up spills at once and treat appropriately.
• Brush or vacuum natural-fibre floor coverings regularly to prevent dirt from breaking down the fibres.

Previous pages:
1. Woven-paper floor covering.
2. Bamboo matting.
This page:
1. Felt and cotton textiles.
2. Interlocking felt floor mats.
Overleaf:
1.–4. Fabric made of hemp in various weights and weaves.
5. Coir. 6. Jute. 7. Coir.
8. Jute. 9. Seagrass.
10. Sisal. 11. Seagrass.
12. Sisal. 13. Coir carpeting laid wall to wall. 14. Barkcloth.
15.–17. Paper matting in different weaves.

2

1

3

2

4

5

6

7

8

9

10

11

12

13

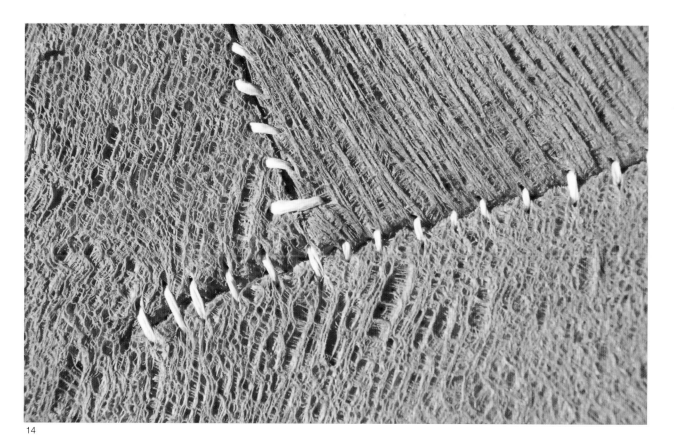

14

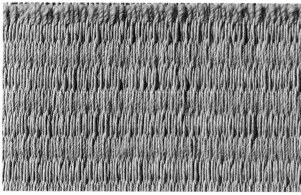

15

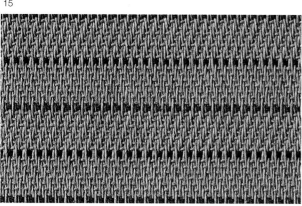

16

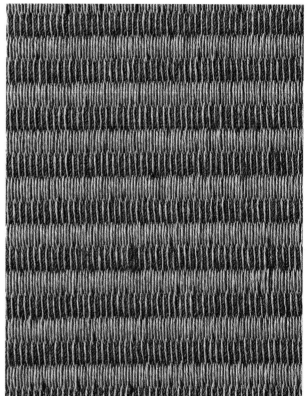

17

1

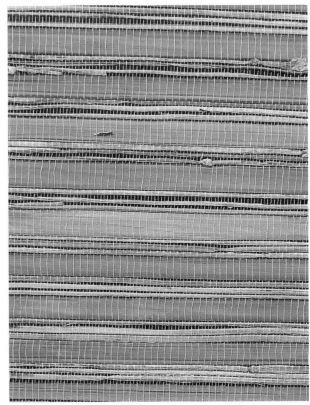

2

natural papers

Most of the paper produced today ultimately comes from trees. However, paper recycling is well established and successful, and recycled paper is increasingly used in newspapers, magazines, books, kitchen paper towels, toilet paper and even wallpaper.

As in the case of natural textiles, different papers can also be produced from a wide variety of grasses and other fibres. In many instances, these are hand-woven to produce a pleasingly textured product that gives definition and character to the interior.

Types of natural papers
• **Arrowroot** Derives from a Caribbean plant and produces a narrow ridged weave in evocative neutral shades.
• **Bamboo** Another application for this versatile plant, bamboo strands can be woven into textured paper. Stronger colours are a feature.
• **Jute** Jute can be woven into fine, silky paper and comes in pale neutral shades.
• **Recycled paper** Most wallpaper today is made of recycled paper. Avoid papers that are surface-treated with vinyl to make them water-resistant. Foil-blocked paper is not eco-friendly.
• **Seagrass** Naturally smooth with a raised texture.
• **Sisal** Sisal papers have

a fine weave and a broader range of colours.
• **Wildgrass** The texture of these papers is reed-like, but flatter than seagrass. Darker shades are typical.

Characteristics
• Papers come from renewable, recyclable, sustainable and biodegradable sources.
• As a wall covering, paper allows walls to breathe and helps to maintain even levels of humidity.
• Good textural depth and definition.

Applications
• As a wall covering. Apply with eco adhesives as recommended.
• As coverings for screens, panels and other flat surfaces.

Finish
• No subsequent finishing is required.
• Dust down with a soft brush from time to time.
• Avoid touching papered surfaces to prevent leaving fingermarks.

1. Woven sisal paper.
2. Seagrass paper.
3. Jute paper.
4. Wildgrass paper.
5. Arrowroot paper.
6. Bamboo wallcovering.

3

4

5

6

salvage & reuse

A large proportion of the materials and associated products mentioned in this book, particularly those that are wholly natural in origin, lend themselves to salvage and reuse. Indeed, one of the key questions consumers should ask themselves before committing to a particular type of surface or finish is how that material will be disposed of once it is irredeemably worn or degraded.

As far as recycling materials is concerned, there are several strategies you can adopt. You can choose to obtain used, recycled or second-hand materials as a substitute for new ones. You can minimize material use by replacing only what is necessary and resisting purely cosmetic makeovers. And, finally, you can prolong the life of those materials you do buy by opting for good-quality ones to begin with and taking care of them properly.

Key points
- How readily can a material be recycled, refinished or reused?
- What type of maintenance does it require? Are there natural alternatives to synthetic finishes and cleaners?
- Does the material have a recycled content?
- Could you source the same material second-hand?

Opposite: Retaining original structural elements is good environmental practice.

1

2

recycled materials

Many natural materials lend themselves to reuse. This is particularly true of the harder-wearing types, such as stone, ceramic tile, brick, hardwood and such like. At some point, original building materials salvaged from houses, churches, hospitals, hotels and other sources, become desirable antiques. Well before then, there is a tendency for construction or demolition waste to be treated simply as rubble and dumped in landfill. (See Recycled wood, pages 212–15). Types include:

• Second-hand materials in a variety of formats reclaimed from demolished buildings or other sources – for example, old bricks, stone pavers, tiles, and floorboards. Price and availability will depend on the age and quality of the material and possibly its provenance.

• Reclaimed architectural detailing, fittings and fixtures. Salvage yards are a good source of details such as doors, windows, fireplaces, panelling, mouldings and trim, baths, sinks, basins, ironmongery, door furniture and a host of other interior features. Again, price and availability will depend on quality, style and condition.

• Furniture and furnishings. There is a large and well-established trade in second-hand furniture and furnishings, ranging from valuable and highly sought-after antiques to retro pieces dating from more recent periods. Textiles are the most vulnerable to decay, but there are some outlets that sell unused remnants or offcuts and surplus from the commercial sector. Some local authorities will now collect furniture in decent condition, repair it and sell it on at low prices; similar schemes are in place for working appliances. A number of companies hire out carpet, take it back after it is worn and recycle it into more carpet.

• Materials with a high recycled content. Synthetic materials with a significant recycled content are considered environmentally friendly. Paper and glass are easily recycled. Recycled glass tiles, for example, are produced using a quarter of the energy needed to make cast glass tiles.

3

4

minimizing material use

The attitudes of our disposable society have found their way into our homes. Nowadays, many people redecorate and refurnish and re-equip their houses much more frequently than their parents' or grandparents' generations and often for no more compelling reason than a stylistic change of heart. While our surroundings are only truly comfortable if they express our tastes and please us on both aesthetic and practical levels, there are still ways in which you can cut wastage in this respect.

Strategies include
• Repairing and restoring existing surfaces and finishes wherever possible. Rather than covering existing timber floors with a new floor covering, for example, think about sanding and refinishing them.
• Restrict the use of new materials to what you can see. The carcases of fitted kitchen units, bathroom vanities and fitted storage can be given a fresh face with new doors, drawer fronts and worktops.
• Give your home a facelift with paint, fabric, accessories and other relatively minimal applications of materials. Don't rip everything out and start again.

investing in quality

Eco awareness means taking the long view. When you have a considerable surface area to cover, invest in the best quality you can afford. Short-term, stopgap solutions tend to be supplied by synthetic materials because they are cheaper. However, their production and disposal is extremely costly for the environment.

Good-quality materials, especially natural ones, tend to wear better. Furthermore, once they show the marks of use, their character tends to be enhanced. Worn vinyl has no such charm.

Once you have invested in quality, do spend time and effort on keeping surfaces and finishes in good condition. Regular refinishing and proper maintenance will add years, if not decades, of serviceable life.

1. Salvage yards are a good source of architectural features and detail.
2. Reclaimed kitchen fixtures and fittings.
3. Vintage washbasin.
4. Visit junk shops and similar outlets for second-hand furnishings.

Stockists, Manufacturers, Suppliers

CLASSIC

Wood

Junckers Ltd
Unit A
1 Wheaton Road
Witham
Essex CM8 3UJ
UK
Tel: +44 (0)1376 534 700
www.junckers.com

Second Nature
Kitchen Collection
PO Box 20
Station Road
Aycliffe Industrial Park
Newton Aycliffe
Co. Durham, DL5 6XJ
UK
Tel: +44 (0)1325 505 539
www.sncollection.co.uk
For details of the 200
Second Nature Kitchen
outlets across the UK
and Ireland telephone
or visit the website

Stone

Fired Earth
3 Twyford Mill
Oxford Road
Adderbury
Oxfordshire OX17 3SX
UK

Tel: +44 (0)845 366 0400
www.firedearth.com

Second Nature
Kitchen Collection
PO Box 20
Station Road
Aycliffe Industrial Park
Newton Aycliffe
Co. Durham, DL5 6XJ
UK
Tel: +44 (0)1325 505 539
www.sncollection.co.uk
For details of the 200
Second Nature Kitchen
outlets across the UK
and Ireland telephone
or visit the website

Brick & ceramic

Architectural
Ceramics (UK) Ltd
Ceramic House
Monarch Industrial Park
198 Kings Road
Tyseley
Birmingham B11 2AP
UK
Tel: +44 (0)121 706 6456
www.actiles.co.uk
Ceramic and mosaic
tiles

Fired Earth
3 Twyford Mill
Oxford Road
Adderbury
Oxfordshire OX17 3SX
UK
Tel: +44 (0)845 366 0400

www.firedearth.com
Terracotta, ceramic,
mosaic and quarry tiles

Ibstock Brick Ltd
Parkhouse Factory
Speedwell Road
Parkhouse Industrial
    Estate East
Newcastle-under-Lyme
Staffordshire ST5 7RZ
UK
Tel: +44 (0)1782 561 332
For your nearest sales
office call: 0870 903 4007
www.ibstock.com
Brick

Linoleum

Forbo-Flooring
PO Box 1
Kirkcaldy
Fife, KY1 2SB
UK
Tel: +44 (0)1592 643 777
For UK stockists call:
0800 731 2369
www.forbo-
flooring.co.uk

Vinyl

Armstrong Floor
Products Europe
Internet Home Team UK
Fleck Way
Teesside Industrial
    Estate
Thornaby On Tees
TS17 9JT

UK
Tel: +44 (0)1642 763 224
www.armstrong.com

Harvey Maria Ltd
Acorn House
74–94 Cherry Orchard
    Road
Croydon
Surrey CR0 6BA
UK
Tel: +44 (0)845 680 1231
+44 (0)20 8688 4700
www.harveymaria.co.uk

Carpet

Craigie Stockwell
Carpets Ltd
81 York Street
London W1H 1QH
UK
Tel: +44 (0)20 7224 8380
www.craigiestockwell
carpets.com

Jacaranda Carpets Ltd
Waterloo Lodge
Braybrooke Road
Great Oxendon
Market Harborough
Leicestershire
LE16 8LU
UK
Tel: +44 (0)1858 464 144
www.jacarandacarpets.
com

Rugs

loophouse
88 Southwark Bridge
   Road
London SE1 0EX
UK
Tel: +44 (0)20 7207 7619
www.loophouse.com

Textiles & papers

Designers Guild
267 & 277 Kings Road
London SW3 5EN
UK
Tel: +44 (0)20 7351 5775
For stockists call:
+44 (0)20 7893 7400
www.designersguild.
com

Eijffinger
Postbus 200
2700 AE Zoetermeer
The Netherlands
Tel: +31 (0)79 344 1200
Export Sales Department:
+31 (0)79 344 1245
www.eijffinger.nl

Elanbach
Llangoed Hall
Llyswen
Brecon
Powys LD3 0YP
UK
Tel: +44 (0)1874 754 631
www.elanbach.com

Ian Mankin
109 Regents Park
   Road
London NW1 8UR
UK
Tel: +44 (0)20 7722 0997
www.ianmankin.com

Jocelyn Warner
3–4 Links Yard
Spelman Street
London E1 5LX
UK
Tel: +44 (0)20 7375 3754
www.jocelynwarner.com

loophouse
88 Southwark Bridge
   Road
London SE1 0EX
UK
Tel: +44 (0)20 7207 7619
www.loophouse.com

Melin Tregwynt
Castlemorris
Haverfordwest
Pembrokeshire
SA62 5UX
UK
Tel: +44 (0)1348 891 225
For mail order call:
+ 44 (0)1348 891 644
www.melintregwynt.
co.uk

Romo Ltd
Lowmoor Road
Kirkby-in-Ashfield
Nottinghamshire
NG17 7DE
UK
Tel: +44 (0)1623 756 699
www.romofabrics.com

CONTEMPORARY

Concrete

**Cast Advanced
Concretes Ltd**
Blackhill Road
Holton Heath Industrial
   Estate
Poole
Dorset BH16 6LS
UK
Tel: +44 (0)870 241 8171
www.castadvanced
concretes.com
Advanced cast
concrete

Jethro Macey
The Design Centre
Tremough
Penryn TR10 9EZ
Cornwall
Tel: +44 (0)7813 930 219
www.jethromacey.com
Blocks, tiles, panels
and slabs

Litracon Bt
Tanya 832
H-6640 Csongrád
Hungary
Tel: +36 30 255 1648
www.litracon.hu
Translucent concrete

Flowcrete Europe Ltd
The Flooring
Technology Centre
Booth Lane
Moston
Sandbach
Cheshire CW11 3QF
UK
Tel: +44 (0)1270 753 000
www.flowcrete.com
Terrazzo

Metal

The Cloth Clinic
The Old Rectory
Sheldon
Near Honiton
Devon EX14 4QU
UK
Tel: +44 (0)1404 841 350
www.clothclinic.com
Metal mesh and metal
fabrics

Gooding Aluminium Ltd
1 British Wharf
Landmann Way
London SE14 5RS
UK
Tel: +44 (0)20 8692 2255
www.goodingalum.com
Sheet metal

H & B Wire
Fabrications Ltd
30–32 Tatton Court
Kingsland Grange
Woolston
Warrington
Cheshire WA1 4RR
UK
Tel: +44 (0)1925 819 515
www.hbwf.co.uk
Metal mesh and metal
fabrics

Glass

Axolotl Group
6/73 Beauchamp Road
Matraville
NSW 2036
Australia
Tel: +61 2 9666 1207
www.axolotl-group.com
Strengthened glass,
decorative glass and
architectural textured
glass

Lumaglass™
Ashbury House
6 Ashton Road
Rutherglen
Glasgow G73 1UB
UK
Tel: +44 (0)141 613 6060
www.lumaglass.co.uk
Profiled glass systems

Luxcrete Ltd
Premier House
Disraeli Road
Park Royal
London NW10 7BT
UK
Tel: +44 (0)20 8965 7292
www.luxcrete.co.uk
Glass blocks

Pilkington Group Ltd
Prescot Road
St Helens
Merseyside WA10 3TT
UK
Tel: +44 (0)1744 28882
www.pilkington.com
Strengthened glass,
decorative glass and
architectural textured
glass

Reglit Glass
Ashbury House
6 Ashton Road
Rutherglen
Glasgow G73 1UB
UK
Tel: +44 (0)141 613 6060
www.reglit.com
Profiled glass systems

Saint-Gobain Glass
Les Miroirs
18, avenue d'Alsace
92400 Courbevoie
France
Tel: +33 1 47 62 30 00
www.saint-gobain.com
Decorative glass and
architectural textured
glass

Solutia Inc.
PO Box 66760
St Louis,
   MO 63166-6760
USA
Tel: +1 (314) 674 1000
www.solutia.com
Coloured laminated
safety glass

Composites

3Form
2300 South 2300
West, Suite B
Salt Lake City
Utah 84119
USA
Tel: +1 801 649 2500
www.3-form.com
Sheet resin

Corian®
Tel: 0800 962 116
www.corian.com

Formica Ltd
Coast Road
North Shields
Tyne & Wear
NE29 8RE
UK
Tel: +44 (0)191 259 3000
www.formica.co.uk
Decorative laminate

Futimis Systems
PO Box 76655
Atlanta, GA 30358
USA
Tel: +1 404 255 3525
www.futimis.com
Sheet resin

Perspex® from Lucite®
PO Box 34
Darwen
Lancs BB3 1QB
UK
Tel: +44 (0)1254 874 000
www.lucite.com
Acrylic

Second Nature
Kitchen Collection
PO Box 20
Station Road
Aycliffe Industrial Park
Newton Aycliffe
Co. Durham, DL5 6XJ
UK
Tel: +44 (0)1325 505 539
www.sncollection.co.uk
Composite stone.
For details of the 200
Second Nature Kitchen
outlets across the UK
and Ireland telephone
or visit the website

Rubber

Dalsouple
Showground Road
Bridgwater
Somerset TA6 6AJ
UK
Tel: +44 (0)1278 727 777
www.dalsouple.com
Natural rubber

Tiles

Architectural
Ceramics (UK) Ltd
Ceramic House
Monarch Industrial Park
198 Kings Road
Tyseley
Birmingham B11 2AP
UK
Tel: +44 (0)121 706 6456
www.actiles.co.uk
Glass tiles

Blackstock Leather
Inc.
13452 Kennedy Road
Stouffville
Ontario
Canada L4A 7X5
Tel: +1 905 888 7070
www.blackstockleather.
com
Leather

Cuoioarredo
division of Cuoificio
Bisonte s.p.a.
Via Masini, 36
56029 S. Croce
sull'Amo (Pisa)
Italy
Tel: +39 0571 30036
www.cuoioarredo.it
Leather

Dominic Crinson
27 Camden Passage
London N1 8EA
UK
Tel: +44 (0)20 7704 6538
www.crinson.com
Photoceramics and
digital tiles

Droog
Staalstraat 7a–7b
1011 JJ Amsterdam
The Netherlands
Tel: +31 (0)20 523 5050
www.droogdesign.nl
Functional tiles

Effepimarmi S.r.l.
Via del Commercio
    Nord 69
56034 Casciana Terme
    (PI)
Italy
Tel: +39 0587 646 404
www.effepimarmi.it
Riverstone, pebble and
stone tiles

Fired Earth
3 Twyford Mill
Oxford Road
Adderbury
Oxfordshire OX17 3SX
UK
Tel: +44 (0)845 366 0400
www.firedearth.com
Glass tiles

Natural Stone Outlet
Tel: 1 888 848 4537
www.naturalstoneoutlet.
com
Pebble and stone tiles

Royal Tichelaar
Turfmarkt 65
8754 CJ Makkum
The Netherlands
Tel: +31 (0)515 23 13 41
www.tichelaar.nl
Photoceramics and
digital tiles

Villiglas GmbH
Sittersdorf 42
9133 Miklauzhof
Austria
Tel: +43 4237 23033 111
www.villiglas.at
Glass tiles

SMART

Reactive glass

SGG Privalite
Saint-Gobain Glass
Les Miroirs
18, avenue d'Alsace
92400 Courbevoie
France
Tel: +33 1 47 62 30 00
www.sggprivalite.com
Liquid crystal glazing

Smartglass
International
PO Box 293
Waterlooville
Hampshire PO7 9AA
UK
Tel: +44 (0)2392 250 660
www.smartglass
international.com
Liquid crystal glazing

Pilkington Group Ltd
Prescot Road
St Helens
Merseyside WA10 3TT
UK
Tel: +44 (0)1744 28882
www.pilkington.com
Self-cleaning glass

Tiles

Gruppe RE
Gladbacherstrasse 24
50672 Köln
Germany
Tel: +49 (0)221 95 45 101
www.gruppe-re.de
Photoluminescent
glass tiles

Keiko Altin Oyabu
www.keikooyabu.com
Repositionable gel tiles

Steuler Fliesen GmbH
Industriestraße 77
D-75417 Mühlacker
Germany
Tel: +49 (0)70 41 8 01 110
www.steuler-fliesen.de
LED tiles

Textiles

Freedom Of Creation
Hobbemakade 85 hs
1071 XP Amsterdam
The Netherlands
Tel: +31 (0)20 675 8415
www.freedomof
creation.com
Laser-sintered textiles

International Fashion
Machines
1205 East Pike Street
Suite 2G
Seattle, WA 98112
USA
Tel: +1 206 860 5166
www.ifmachines.com
Programmable electric
textiles

Lily Latifi
11 rue des gardes
75018 Paris
France
Tel: +33 1 42 23 30 86
www.lilylatifi.com
Laser-cut textiles

Loop.pH
8 Springfield House
5 Tyssen Street
London E8 2LY
UK
Tel: +44 (0)20 7812 9188
www.loop.ph
Electroluminescent
fabric

Luminites
c/o 111a–113a
Belgrave Road
Leicester LE4 6AS
UK
Tel: +44 (0)1162 680 822
www.luminites.co.uk
Textiles woven with
optical fibres

Sharon Marston
Studio F31 & F34A
Parkhall Road Trading
    Estate
40 Martell Road
London SE21 8EN
UK
Tel: +44 (0)20 8670 4644
www.sharonmarston.
com
Textiles woven with
optical fibres

Interactive wallpaper

Gruppe RE
Gladbacherstrasse 24
50672 Köln
Germany
Tel: +49 (0)221 95 45 101
www.gruppe-re.de

Rachel Kelly
Interactive Wallpaper™
Unit 4 & 5 Barn Farm
Ratherheath Lane
Bonningate nr Kendal
Cumbria LA8 8JX
UK
Tel: +44 (0)1539 822 511
www.interactivewall
paper.co.uk

Loop.pH
8 Springfield House
5 Tyssen Street
London E8 2LY
UK
Tel: +44 (0)20 7812 9188
www.loop.ph

Interactive flooring

Rogier Sterk
Vijfzinnenstraat 105
6811 LN
Arnhem
The Netherlands
Tel: +31 (0)6 27 48 33 51
www.rogiersterk.nl
Interactive light flooring

Natalie Woolf
PhD(RCA)
c/o InnovationRCA
Royal College of Art
Kensington Gore
London SW7 2EU
UK
Tel: +44 (0)7957 460 149
Email: natalie.woolf@
alumni.rca.ac.uk
www.innovation.rca.ac.
uk/archive/pr_sing.php
?i=3
Interactive light flooring

SUSTAINABLE

Alternatives to wood

Smith & Fong
475 6th Street
San Francisco,
CA 94103
USA
Tel: +1 415 896 0577
Freephone: 866 835
9859
www.plyboo.com
Bamboo and palm

Amorim Flooring (UK)
Tel: +44 (0)1403 710 001
Email: info.ar.uk@
amorim.com
www.wicanders.com
Cork

Recycled decking

Maine Deck
Maine House
54 Meadow Way
Verwood
Dorset BH31 6HG
UK
Tel: +44 (0)8456 123 104
www.maine-deck.co.uk

Eco glass

Pilkington Group Ltd
Prescot Road
St Helens
Merseyside WA10 3TT
UK
Tel: +44 (0)1744 28882
www.pilkington.com

Saint-Gobain Glass
Les Miroirs
18, avenue d'Alsace
92400 Courbevoie
France
Tel: +33 1 47 62 30 00
www.saint-gobain.com

Recycled plastics

Smile Plastics Ltd
Mansion House
Ford
Shrewsbury SY5 9LZ
UK
Tel: +44 (0)1743 850 267
www.smile-
plastics.co.uk
Recycled plastic sheet

Durat®
Huhdantie 4
21140 Rymättylä
Finland
Tel: +358 (0)2 252 1000
www.durat.com

Textiles & papers

Bark Cloth – Europe
Oliver Heintz
Gewerbestr.9
D-79285 Ebringen
Germany
Tel: +49 (0)7664 403 15 60
+49 (0)700 22 75 25 68
www.barktex.com
Barkcloth

Crucial Trading
PO Box 10469
Birmingham B46 1WB
UK
Tel: +44 (0)1562 743 747
www.crucial-
trading.com
Natural fibres

Hemp Fabric UK
Kavella
Bishops Tawton
Barnstaple
Devon EX32 0AP
UK
Tel: +44 (0)1271 314 812
www.hempfabric.co.uk
Hemp

Lily Latifi
11 rue des gardes
75018 Paris
France
Tel: +33 1 42 23 30 86
www.lilylatifi.com
Natural fibres

Urbaneliving
Studio 102
The Light Box
111 Power Road
London W4 5PY
UK
Tel: +44 (0)845 257 2382
www.urbaneliving.co.uk
Natural papers

Salvage & reuse

Baileys
Whitecross Farm
Bridstow
Herefordshire HR9 6JU
UK
Tel: +44 (0)1989 561 931
www.baileyshomeand
garden.com

Index

Figures in italics indicate captions.

Acknowledgements

The publishers would like to thank the following sources for their kind permission to reproduce the photographs in this book:

1 Elanbach; 2 Arcaid/John Edward Linden/Kanner Architects; 4 Serge Brison/Architect: Jöel Claisse; 6–7 images supplied by manufacturers featured in this book; 9 Ray Main/Mainstreamimages/Domus Furniture; 10 Smile Plastics; 12–13 Ray Main/Mainstreamimages/Architects: McDowel & Benedetti; 14 and 17 Architectural Ceramics; 18–19 Ray Main/Mainstreamimages/Kit Grover; 20 Ray Main/Mainstreamimages/concetto@centimetro.net; 20 Junckers; 24 left Serge Brison/Architect: Van Nuffel; 24 right and 25 Second Nature Kitchen Collection; 26 top Junckers; 26 bottom left and bottom right Second Nature Kitchen Collection; 27 top left and top right Junckers; 27 bottom, 28 and 29 top left and top right Second Nature Kitchen Collection; 29 bottom left Istock; 29 bottom right Second Nature Kitchen Collection; 30 left Arcaid/Alan Weintraub; 30 top right and bottom right Istock; 31 Arcaid/Alan Weintraub; 32 Arcaid/Simon Kenny/Architect: Ken Latona; 33 Serge Brison/Architect: Benoit Courtens; 34 Ray Main/Mainstreamimages/Polescuk Architects; 35 Arcaid/John Edward Linden/Kanner Architects; 36 Arcaid/Alberto Piovano/Architect: Marco Romanelli; 37 Ray Main/Mainstreamimages/Architects: McDowel & Benedetti; 39 Arcaid/Simon Kenny; 40 Luxproductions.com; 41 Arcaid/David Churchill/Stickland Coombe Architecture; 42 Serge Brison/Architects: Buelens-Vanderlinden; 44 and 45 Second Nature Kitchen Collection; 46 left Arcaid/ Richard Bryant; 46 top right, right of centre and bottom right Second Nature Kitchen Collection; 47 Serge Brison/ Architect: Jöel Claisse; 48 left Serge Brison/Thermes de Vals/Architect: Peter Zumthor; 48 top right Second Nature Kitchen Collection; 48 bottom right Istock; 49 top left Second Nature Kitchen Collection; 49 top right, centre and bottom Fired Earth; 50 left and bottom right Fired Earth; 50 top right Second Nature Kitchen Collection; 51 Fired Earth; 52 Arcaid/Richard Powers/Architect: Daniel Marshall; 53 Second Nature Kitchen Collection; 55 Arcaid/Richard Bryant/Architects: Terry Farrell & Partners for Berkeley Homes; 56 Ray Main/Mainstreamimages/ Design: Paul Priestman; 58 and 59 Ibstock Brick Ltd; 60 Ray Main/Mainstreamimages/Kit Grover; 61 Ray Main/Mainstreamimages; 62 Fired Earth; 63 Redcover ©

Alex Ramsay; 64–67 Fired Earth; 68–71 Forbo; 72 top left and top right Armstrong World Industries, Inc; 72 bottom left and bottom right Harvey Maria; 73 top left and top right Armstrong World Industries, Inc.; 73 bottom left and bottom right Harvey Maria; 75 Armstrong World Industries, Inc.; 76 Redcover © James Balston; 79 Redcover © Paul Massey; 80 Jacaranda Carpets; 81 Craigie Stockwell Carpets; 82–85 loophouse; 86 and 88 left Designers Guild; 88 right Melin Tregwynt; 89 left Elanbach; 89 right and 90 Designers Guild; 91 Melin Tregwynt; 92 left Paul Massey/ Mainstreamimages; 92 right Romo; 93 top left Jocelyn Warner; 93 top right, bottom left and bottom right Eijffinger; 94 top loophouse; 94 bottom left and bottom right and 95 Eijffinger; 96–97 Trevor Mein/Meinphoto; 99 Redcover © Henry Wilson; 100 Serge Brison/Architect: Bruno Albert; 102 Serge Brison/Architect: Jöel Claisse; 103 Serge Brison/Architects: Wastchenko et Jongen; 104 Jethro Macey; 105 Arcaid/John Edward Linden/Kanner Architects; 106–107 Litracon; 108–109 Cast Advanced Concrete; 110 and 111 Flowcrete; 112 Arcaid/Eugeni Pons/Architect: Anne Bugugnani; 114 left Arcaid/Alan Weintraub/Architect: Albert Frey; 114 top right Arcaid/Nicholas Kane/Architect: Acanthus Ferguson Mann; 114 bottom right Serge Brison/ Architects: Buelens-Vanderlinden; 115 Arcaid/Eugeni Pons/ Architect: RCR Arquitectes; 116 left Serge Brison/ Architect: Jöel Claisse; 116 right Serge Brison/Architect: Bruno Corbisier; 117 left and top right Arcaid/Nicholas Kane/Architect: Niall McLaughlin; 117 bottom right Serge Brison/Architect: Van Nuffel; 118 left Nicholas Kane/ Architects: Buschow Henley; 118 left Redcover © Jake Fitzjones; 119 left Redcover © Ken Hayden; 119 top tight Redcover © Graham Atkins-Hughes; 119 bottom right Serge Brison/Architect: Bruno Corbisier; 120 Janet Stoyal; 121 Serge Brison/Casa Camper, Barcelona/Architect: Ferdinando Amat; 122 Serge Brison/Architect: Angel Luis Lorenzo Medel; 124 left and right Serge Brison/Architect: Francois Van Eetvelde; 125 top Serge Brison/Architect: Erick Van Egeraat; 125 bottom Axolotl Group; 126 Serge Brison/Solutia Glass; 127 top left, top right and bottom left Axolotl Group; 127 bottom right Pilkington Group Ltd; 128 left and top right Serge Brison/Solutia Glass; 128 bottom right Serge Brison/Architects: Bouquelle-Popof; 129 Axolotl Group; 130 Lumaglass™; 131 Graven Images & Keith Hunter – Reglit Glass Architecture; 132 Darren Chung/ Mainstreamimages/Ripples Bathrooms; 133 Arcaid/Richard Bryant/Architect: John Young; 134 Serge Brison/Casa Camper, Barcelona/Architect: Ferdinando Amat; 135 left Arcaid/David Churchill/Architect: McKeown Alexander;

135 top right Darren Chung/Mainstreamimages/Ice Cube Design; 135 bottom right Arcaid/Nicholas Kane/Belsize Architects; 136 3Form; 138 top left Lucite International; 138 bottom left 3Form; 138 right Redcover © Graham Atkins-Hughes; 139 Luxproductions.com; 140 top 'Block' in DuPont™ Corian®, produced by Planit, design Simone Micheli; 140 bottom 'Quadro' in DuPont™ Corian®, produced by Respect, design Francesco Lucchese; 141 top left Second Nature Kitchen Collection; 141 right Kitchen in DuPont™ Corian®, private home (UK), design Ellis Williams Architects; 141 bottom left 'Matrix' kitchen in DuPont™ Corian®, produced by Varenna, design Paulo Piva; 142 and 143 Formica; 144 and 145 3Form; 146 Ray Main/Mainstreamimages; 148 left Dalsouple/Deacons Law Consultancy, Australia/Photographer: Robert Frith; 148 top right and bottom right and 149 Dalsouple; 150–151 Nick Kane/Architects: Buschow Henley; 152 Architectural Ceramics; 154 Cuoioarredo; 155 Redcover © Winfried Heinze; 156 and 157 Dominic Crinson; 158 and 159 Droog; 160 and 161 top left and top right Riverstone; 161 bottom left and bottom right Natural Stone Outlet; 162 and 163 top left, top right, below centre left and below centre right Fired Earth; 163 below centre left and below centre right Architectural Ceramics; 164–165 International Fashion Machines, Inc.; 167 Loop.pH; 168 Dorchester Hotel/Saint-Gobain; 170–171 David Spero/Seth Stein Architects; 172 and 173 top Pilkington Group Ltd/Photographer: Eric Sierens; 173 bottom Pilkington Group Ltd/Photographer: Peter Hyatt; 174 Steuler-fliesen.de; 176 and 177 Keiko Altin Oyabu; 178 and 179 Gruppe RE; 180–183 Steuler-fliesen.de; 184 Loop.pH; 186 and 187 Freedom of Creation; 188 Lily Latifi; 189 International Fashion Machines; 190 and 191 Loop.pH; 192 and 193 top and bottom left Sharon Marston; 193 bottom right Luminites; 194 left Loop.pH; 194 top right Gruppe RE; 194 bottom right Rachel Kelly Interactive Wallpapers™; 195 top left Gruppe RE; 195 top right, bottom left and bottom right Rachel Kelly Interatctive Wallpapers™; 196 and 197 Loop.pH; 198 Rogier Sterk; 200–201 Arcaid/Martine Hamilton Knight/Architect: Associated Architects; 203 Crucial Trading; 204 Benny Chan Photography, courtesy of Smith & Fong Durapalm; 206 left and right John Sutton Photography, courtesy of Smith & Fong Plyboo; 207 top left and right Ray Main/Mainstreamimages; 207 bottom left Photo courtesy of Smith & Fong Plyboo; 208 Benny Chan Photography, courtesy of Smith & Fong Durapalm; 209 Photography courtesy of Smith & Fong Durapalm; 210 and 211 Photography: Verne/Architect: Axel Ghyssaert; 212 Redcover © Ed Reeve; 214 Garden Picture Library/Lynn Keddie; 215 top Garden Picture Library/Mark Bolton; 215 bottom Marianne Majerus; 216 Redcover © James Balston; 218 left Ray Main/Mainstreamimages; 218 right Darren Chung/Mainstreamimages/Architect: David Gregory; 219 Arcaid/Lewis Gasson/Architects: Designers Collaborative Ltd; 220 left Ray Main/Mainstreamimages; 220 right Redcover © Anthony Harrison; 221 Arcaid/Marc Gerritsen/Vision Design Studio, Jeff Chao; 222 Klein Dytham Architecture/Katsuhisa Kida; 224 and 225 Smile Plastics Ltd; 226 left and right Durat®; 227 top Durat®/Photographers: Matthijs van Roon & Mandy Pieper/Architect: Piet Boon; 227 bottom left and bottom right Durat®; 228–231 Crucial Trading; 235 and 236 Crucial Trading; 237 top Barkcloth Europe; 238 and 239 Urbane Living; 240 Serge Brison/Architects: Baneton-Garino; 242 left Arcaid/Richard Powers; 242 right Ray Main/Mainstreamimages/Alistair Hendy Design; 243 left Luxproductions.com; 243 right Redcover © Dan Duchars.

Editorial Director Anne Furniss
Creative Director Helen Lewis
Designer Ros Holder
Project Editor Zia Mattocks
Picture Researcher Emily Hedges
Production Ruth Deary

This paperback edition published in 2009 by
Quadrille Publishing Limited
Alhambra House
27–31 Charing Cross Road
London WC2H 0LS
www.quadrille.co.uk

First published in 2007 as *Surface & Finish*

Reprinted in 2011
10 9 8 7 6 5 4 3 2

Cataloguing in Publication Data: a catalogue record for
this book is available from the British Library.

ISBN-13: 978 184400 709 7

Printed in China